A CELEBRATION OF
IRELAND

Janice Anderson

PHOTOGRAPHY BY DAVID LYONS

CHARTWELL
BOOKS, INC.

Published in 2008 by
CHARTWELL BOOKS, INC.
A division of BOOK SALES, INC.
114 Northfield Avenue
Edison, New Jersey 08837
USA

**Copyright © 2008 Regency
House Publishing Limited**
Niall House
24–26 Boulton Road
Stevenage, Hertfordshire
SG1 4QX, UK

For all editorial enquiries please contact
Regency House Publishing at
www.regencyhousepublishing.com

ISBN-13: 978-0-7858-2202-8
ISBN-10: 0-7858-2202-X

Printed in China

All photographs supplied by
DAVID LYONS

Except for: Pages 30, 31 right, 36, 39, 46, 48,
49, 51, 53, 56, 57 left, 58, 59, 63 right, 65, 77
right, 82, 90, 95, 96, 98, 101, 104, 106, 114,
119, 121, 122, 124, 125, 126 left, 131, 136, 137
left, 138 bottom, 140, 146, 150 right, 151, 176
left, 178 left, 180, 182 both, 239, 242, 243, 245,
257, 258, 259, 304, 306 both, 433.
Supplied by Don Sutton International
Picture Library

CONTENTS

INTRODUCTION

BELOW: Devenish Island round tower and monastery buildings, Co. Fermanagh.

OPPOSITE LEFT: Fishing boats at Killybegs, Donegal.

A Hundred Thousand Welcomes – *Céad Mile Fáilte'* – is how they greet you all over Ireland. It is a neat summing-up of everything the visitor has come to expect of the island: a warmly relaxed welcome from a friendly people, famed for their way with words and possessed of more than a touch of the romantically exotic, inherited from the Gaels (Celts), who were the first to bring true civilization and a rich culture to the island.

The island of Ireland is the third largest in Europe and the second largest of the British Isles. It lies on the western edge of the great European land mass, the shape of its eastern edge showing how it was originally joined to Britain, while its western coast thrusts out into the Atlantic Ocean. It is not very big, being just over 300 miles (480km) from top to bottom and measuring about 170 miles (275km) at its widest point.

OPPOSITE: The weir on the River Boyne at Slane, County Meath.

LEFT: Georgian townhouses in Merrion Square, Dublin.

PAGE 12: Thoroughbred brood mares with their foals at the Irish National Stud Farm at Tully near Kildare, where champion racehorses are born.

PAGE 13: St. Fiachra's Garden at the Irish National Stud, Tully, Kildare.

INTRODUCTION

BELOW & RIGHT: Powerscourt, a Georgian mansion near Enniskerry, County Wicklow.

OPPOSITE: Carrick-a-Rede, a rope suspension bridge near Ballintoy, County Antrim.

It is an island with few natural resources: no oil, some coal in Tipperary, Europe's largest lead and zinc mine in County Meath, and large stretches of peat bog, still an important source of natural fuel; this in itself was the result of the unchecked felling of primeval forest which, by about 1700, left Ireland the most sparsely wooded country in Europe. But Ireland is also one of the loveliest and most appealing of Europe's islands, blessed with a mild

OPPOSITE: *Poulnabrone, literally the 'hole of sorrows', is a prehistoric dolmen portal tomb, situated on The Burren limestone pavement near Caherconnell in County Clare.*

LEFT: *The Bunratty Folk Park adjoins Bunratty Castle, County Clare. Here, traditional Irish folk-dancing takes place in front of the village pub.*

PAGE 18: *White quartzite scree lying on the slopes of Errigal, Donegal's highest mountain at 2,457ft (749m).*

PAGE 19: *The view to the south-west down the Owenea river at Ardara in County Donegal. It is one of the best spots for salmon-fishing in the county.*

climate because of the Gulf Stream. There is a high rainfall, particularly in the west, which accounts for the glorious green of much of the countryside, for which Ireland is justly known as the 'Emerald Isle'.

By far the larger of the two states sharing the island, the other being Northern Ireland, which is part of Great Britain, the Republic of Ireland is one of the boom economies of the European Union, with a success built on fast-growing industry, trade and investment. But it is still very much a rural country, offering a haven of tranquillity far from the bustle of early 21st-century city life.

A main reason for the island's predominantly rural aspect is that it is generally underpopulated, although this has been changing in recent years. In a land where the population had already been greatly reduced by two centuries of emigration, caused in part by choice and in part by grim necessity, there has also been a move away from the countryside and into the towns and cities. More than a third of the Republic's population, which is small by European standards, lives in or around Dublin, while Belfast, the largest city in Northern Ireland, also has by far the largest concentration, with almost a quarter of the Province's total population.

The Ireland of the imagination, the quiet land of fields and thatched cottages, still manages to surprise visitors with the great variety of its contrasting scenery. True, there are the green valleys,

OPPOSITE: The peaceful, unspoilt beach at Culdaff on the Inishowen Peninsula, County Donegal.

LEFT: The Silver Strand lies south of Glencolumbcille on the Slieve League Peninsula at the south-west point of Donegal.

PAGE 22: The harbour and Dominican convent, an imposing Gothic building, at Portstewart, County Londonderry, Northern Ireland.

PAGE 23: John Behan's bronze 'Coffin Ship', a memorial sculpture to Irish emigrants escaping from the Famine. It is situated at Clew Bay near Westport, County Mayo.

RIGHT: The famous 'head' descends a pint of Guinness. The stout is referred to as 'the black stuff', and is Ireland's favourite tipple.

FAR RIGHT: An enamel sign outside a bar in Kerry, advertising Jameson's famous Irish whiskey.

OPPOSITE: Tralee's Rose Garden, in County Kerry, looks splendid each August during the Rose of Tralee Festival, a celebration of female beauty that attracts competitors from all over the world.

watered by great rivers and pretty streams, like something out of a Hollywood movie, but there are also the wild places, the limestone country of The Burren and the Aran Islands, the strange basalt rock formations of the Giant's Causeway on northern Antrim's dramatic coast, and the wind-swept remoteness of much of the mountain country to the west, where belief in the 'little people' of

Celtic myth still survives and where the majority of people still speak the Irish language.

Water, in thousands of lakes and hundreds of rivers, streams and waterways, gives the countryside a softly-shining beauty, unique to Ireland, and adds greatly to its attraction as a place where you can take a holiday and get away from it all. It is possible to pass quiet hours completely undisturbed, fishing in rivers and lakes teeming with fish, or watching the birdlife that congregates in great numbers along their banks and shores.

If the faster pace of town and city life is something you can't altogether do without, then Ireland can offer that, too, in splendid variety, from the mixture of Georgian elegance, modern style and bohemian life which is Dublin at the beginning of a new century, to the medieval mazes with more than a touch of the modern that characterize towns like Kilkenny, Galway and Waterford.

Belfast, too, having been plagued by the 'Troubles' which have dominated life in Northern Ireland for so long and which are themselves the terrible legacy of centuries of bitter strife and tragedy throughout the island, still retains its heart and a solid core of Victorian solidity, and the city's new Waterfront Hall, a splendidly Modernist, predominantly glass concert hall, built on the banks of the River Lagan, is seen by many as a hopeful look into a happier future.

OPPOSITE: Looking north-west over Lower Lough Erne from the Cliffs of Magho in County Fermanagh.

LEFT: Double the luck! A shamrock of horseshoes, seen on a door at Slea Head in County Kerry.

PAGE 28: Dairy cattle in Antrim, Northern Ireland.

PAGE 29: The west face of the Celtic Christian High Cross of Ardboe, located on a small hillock close to the western shore of Lough Neagh, Tyrone.

CHAPTER ONE

DUBLIN

RIGHT: Tucked behind an archway off Lower Bridge Street, the Brazen Head is said to be the oldest bar in Dublin – even in the whole of Ireland; there has been an inn on the site since the end of the 12th century, although the present building dates from the 1600s.

OPPOSITE LEFT: Kennedy's Bar on George's Quay is on the south side of Liffey Docks.

OPPOSITE RIGHT: Looking west up the River Liffey: a view dominated by several of the 14 bridges which cross the Liffey in Dublin.

Dublin, in the Republic of Ireland, is one of the fastest-growing capital cities in Europe. It is also a gracious city and a compact one, offering many attractions within walking distance of one another that makes it one of Europe's most popular tourist destinations. Dublin has grown fast in recent decades, its suburbs overspilling into the surrounding County Dublin. It is the largest urban area in Ireland and it is estimated that the Greater Dublin area will have a population of 2.1 million by 2021. This has forced it to confront many of the problems of 21st-century urban living, including inner-city deprivation and drug abuse. But even if Dublin appears to share many of the positive as well as the negative characteristics of any great city, it undoubtedly has an atmosphere of energy and dynamism, born no doubt of the inevitable spin-off between traditional conservatism and youthful, cosmopolitan get-up-and-go that make it uniquely attractive among the great cities of the world.

At first glance, today's Dublin could be seen as typical of any modern city, full of discos and clubs, cafés, restaurants and boutiques (providing the designer labels so essential to today's international consumer society), and a good sprinkling of estate agent's boards, evidence of a boom in the property market; but it exists on the foundation of a centuries-long history that is still evident in many parts of the modern city.

Dublin, the heart and mainspring of County Dublin, is superbly situated on Dublin Bay at the mouth of the River Liffey, with the

Dublin is famous for its brightly painted front doors. These attractive examples adorn Merrion Street's fine Georgian townhouses.

Wicklow Mountains making a fine backdrop to the south. It is a setting that has attracted people since prehistoric times; in fact, a map by the second-century astronomer and geographer, Ptolemy, clearly shows that a settlement known as Eblana was established on the Liffey.

CELTS, VIKINGS AND ANGLO-NORMANS

St. Patrick may have come here in the mid-fifth century, and the Norwegian Vikings certainly left their subarctic homes to descend on the British Isles some 400 years later, when, in around AD 840, they ousted the pre-existing Celts and established a trading settlement of their own on the southern banks of the Liffey.

The Viking's name for their riverside settlement derived from the Celtic words for 'Dark Pool' (*Dubh Linn*) and the name has endured, although the name for the Celtic settlement on the northern bank of the Liffey, with which Dublin eventually merged, *Baile Atha Cliath*, meaning 'town of the hurdle ford', remains the Irish name for Dublin to this day. The Viking hold on Dublin lasted until the mighty Irish warrior king, Brian Boru, defeated the invaders at the Battle of Clontarf in 1014.

The Anglo-Normans in England began to turn covetous eyes towards Ireland in the 12th century, when a call for help from one of the several kings then ruling Ireland, who had been turned off his throne by a neighbouring ruler, was too good an opportunity for them to miss. In 1170, the first of the Plantagenet kings of England, Henry II, sent in a force of Welsh knights, led by Richard de Clare, known as Strongbow, to help the ex-king of Leinster who, in turn, swore an oath of fealty to Henry. Strongbow established himself in Ireland, rather too strongly for Henry's liking, and the king set up his own court in Dublin, extending his rule over most of Leinster. From then on, until the 20th century, Dublin was the main base for English influence in Ireland, being firmly at the heart of both political and social life.

The small town began to expand in the 17th century, reaching its heyday in the following century. This was when the building of what is still called Georgian Dublin began, along with the establishment of Dublin as a major centre of brewing, Arthur Guinness founding his famous brewery at St. James's Gate on the Liffey in 1759.

With the conceding of autonomy to the Irish parliament in 1783, Dublin blossomed into a centre of fashionable society, only to see it wane after the Irish Uprising of 1798 caused William Pitt to push through the reunion of the British and Irish parliaments in 1801. By the end of the 19th century, Dublin was very much a quiet Irish town, with strongly Irish cultural movements playing increasingly important roles in the life of the city and of the wider Ireland beyond.

By this time, the British viceroy had moved out of Dublin Castle and taken up court in a grand residence in Phoenix Park to the west of the city and one of the largest urban parks in Europe.

OPPOSITE: A relic of Dublin's 18th-century heyday, the magnificent neo-Classical Custom House on Custom House Quay, stretches along the north bank of the River Liffey between Butt Bridge and the Talbot Memorial Bridge.

*RIGHT & OPPOSITE RIGHT:
Two views of what is popularly
known as the Ha'penny Bridge,
because of the toll that was levied
on it until 1919. A symbol of
Dublin, the Ha'penny Bridge
(officially the Wellington Bridge
after the 'Iron Duke') was built in
1816, the year after the Irish-born
Duke of Wellington's victory over
Napoleon at Waterloo. Cast at
Coalbrookdale in Shropshire in
England, the bridge was the only
pedestrian bridge spanning the
Liffey until the new Millennium
Bridge, built further upstream, was
opened in 2000.*

*OPPOSITE LEFT: A wall plaque
marking the birthplace of the Duke
of Wellington in Merrion Street,
Dublin.*

When the Irish Free State, later the Republic, came into being, Dublin, naturally enough, was its capital and its heart, with the viceroy's house becoming the official residence of the presidents of Ireland.

The infamous Kilmainham Jail, also in the western suburbs of Dublin, south of Phoenix Park and the Liffey, was opened in 1795 and was used to house many political prisoners, including Charles Stewart Parnell and Eamon de Valera. It is now empty but preserved as a grim museum and symbol of the struggle for Irish independence.

RIGHT: Bust of Michael Collins in Archbishop Ryan Park, Merrion Square. An Irish nationalist leader and a member of Parliament for Sinn Fein, Collins was one of the negotiators, with Arthur Griffiths, of the Anglo-Irish Treaty of 1821 that created the partition of Ireland and the Irish Free State. He was assassinated by republican extremists the following year.

OPPOSITE: Designed mainly by James Gandon, the Four Courts, completed in 1802 on a fine site on the north bank of the Liffey, houses the four courts of justice making up the Irish judicial system: Common Pleas, Chancery, Exchequer and King's Bench. The building has excellent sculpture by Edward Smyth; on the main pediment Moses is flanked by Justice and Mercy with Wisdom and Authority also present. The superb building was carefully restored after it was severely damaged during the Irish Civil War.

HISTORIC DUBLIN IN TODAY'S CITY

The early history of Dublin, when Celtic and Viking settlements were established on either side of the Liffey, is still evident in the present-day city, spreading away from both banks of the river, which is spanned by a fine collection of bridges, including the splendid O'Connell Bridge. Pause for a moment in the centre of the bridge and look downstream, when you will see one of the finest views of Dublin, including the span of the delicately slender Ha'penny Bridge.

The city north of the Liffey, bisected by the wide ribbon of O'Connell Street, named after the 'Liberator' Daniel O'Connell, is where the louder, more down-to-earth and sometimes more raucous aspects of Dublin life become apparent. The historic General Post Office, at the centre of the Easter Rising of 1916, and the Abbey Theatre, scene of Ireland's great theatrical revival and the country's National Theatre, are both in this area, as is the Dublin Writers' Museum, housed in two Georgian buildings in Parnell Square. The square, named after Charles Parnell, one of the heroes of the Irish independence movement, was originally called Rutland Square and was one of the first Georgian squares to be built in Dublin.

On the south bank of the river is most of what remains of Dublin's 18th-century heyday, when all that was most cultured and most fashionable in Ireland was centred round Dublin Castle, Trinity College, Leinster House and the gracious Georgian streets

and squares, also the splendid St. Stephen's Green, where the houses of the well-heeled were to be found. Some of the more historic of Dublin's 800 pubs are also on the south side of the Liffey, including Davy Byrne's in Duke Street, off Grafton Street. Here, in James Joyce's *Ulysses*, Leopold Bloom stopped for a sandwich and a glass of burgundy – an event still celebrated in Dublin each Bloomsday (16 June).

Both Leopold Bloom and his creator would be astonished if they could see Grafton Street today, for it has been pedestrianized, giving it quite a Continental air. It is one of Dublin's most fashionable streets, full of shops, department stores and cafés. Its attractions are many, and include lively street entertainers, the oldest of the several Bewley's Oriental Cafés, which are such an attractive part of Dublin's social scene, and a splendid bronze statue of Molly Malone, heroine of the popular song, who stands by her wheelbarrow of 'cockles and mussels, alive, alive-o'.

West of Grafton Street and still on the south, or right, bank of the Liffey, the area known as Temple Bar has become Dublin's answer to Paris's Left Bank. Here is where you will find small experimental theatres, second-hand bookshops, many art galleries and numerous bistros. Development of the area began in a small way, with people taking over disused warehouses; it was all rather shabby and run-down, having once been an area of craftsmen and artisans until creeping industrialization led to their demise. In

recent years it has been gentrified in vaguely 18th-century style, with cobbled streets and old-fashioned street lighting.

Because, as elsewhere in the British Isles, most buildings in Ireland (especially domestic housing before the 17th century) were made of wood or wattle and daub, there is, in fact, very little of the early history of Dublin to be seen in the modern city and insensitive town planning, which began in the 1960s, did little to help: before it could be fully excavated, an extensive Viking site on Wood Quay, near Christ Church Cathedral, eventually disappeared under some unattractive civic building in the 1980s.

OPPOSITE: The O'Connell St. Bridge replaced the original 18th-century Carlisle Bridge in 1880.

LEFT: The O'Connell St. Spire of Dublin (Monument of Light).

BELOW: This 14th-century carving in Christ Church Cathedral is said to be of Strongbow (Richard de Clare).

41

RIGHT: The Shelbourne Hotel. While the central park of St. Stephen's Green is one of three ancient commons in the city, its current layout owes much to the restorations of the 1800s. The Shelbourne Hotel was founded in 1824 by Martin Burke when he acquired three adjoining townhouses overlooking this, Europe's largest garden square. Today, much of it comprises modern buildings, some in a replica Georgian style, with relatively little surviving from the 18th and 19th centuries.

OPPOSITE: The O'Connell Monument and the south end of O'Connell Street, Dublin. Daniel O'Connell was Ireland's premier political leader in the first half of the 19th century, famous for championing the cause of the down-trodden Catholic population. He campaigned for Catholic Emancipation and the repeal of the union between Ireland and Great Britain.

DUBLIN

Three buildings, all south of the Liffey, which can trace their origins back at least to the 12th century, are Dublin Castle and the two cathedrals, St. Patrick's and Christ Church, the Cathedral of the Holy Trinity.

Only the Record Tower, which served as the administration centre for British rule in Ireland between the 18th and 20th centuries, remains of the original Dublin Castle, built in the first half of the 12th century over the 'dark pool' which gave Dublin its name. Most of the Dublin Castle you see today was built and rebuilt over the centuries, though there remains much that is of interest to visitors. The State Apartments include St. Patrick's Hall, where the presidents of the Republic are inaugurated; the Wedgwood Room, decorated in the familiar blue-and-white style of Wedgwood china; and the Throne Room, dominated by a huge throne and last used by Elizabeth II's grandfather, George V.

Christ Church is the older of Dublin's two cathedrals, having been founded by a Norse king, Sitric, in 1038; its magnificent Gothic crypt, crossings and transepts date from two centuries later. The remains of Strongbow (Richard de Clare), who died in 1176, and what is possibly his monument, can be seen in the cathedral, together with a cat in pursuit of a rat (a delightfully Irish touch), which were discovered in the 19th century, stuck in the organ pipes: their 'tomb' is a glass case in which their mummified bodies are displayed.

St. Patrick's Cathedral, a little to the south of Dublin Castle, was founded in 1190 on the legendary site of the baptisms carried out by St. Patrick in the fifth century. The present building dates to 1225, though it has been much altered, rebuilt and enlarged since then. The tomb that most interests visitors, however, is that of Jonathan Swift, author of *Gulliver's Travels* and many other satirical writings, who was Dean of St. Patrick's between 1713 and 1745. The pulpit from which he regularly preached is still preserved in the cathedral, though it is no longer used.

IRELAND'S HERITAGE PRESERVED

In the area of Dublin south of the Liffey, eastwards from the castle and cathedrals, are to be found many of the buildings most intimately connected with Ireland's history and culture.

When the immensely rich Duke of Leinster built his town house, Leinster House, in green fields south of the Liffey, rather than on the more fashionable north side in 1745, many people considered his action to be ill-judged. 'Not so,' said the duke, knowing full well that where he went others would follow, and the green fields were soon full of fine Georgian houses. Today Leinster House is a very important building in Dublin, for it houses Ireland's Parliament. Two great rotundas, added at either side of the house in 1890, now house the entrances to Ireland's National Library and National Museum.

OPPOSITE: Built at the beginning of the 18th century and one of the earliest examples of a galleried church in Dublin, St. Mary's Church (Church of Ireland) ceased to function as a place of worship in 1964, reopening its doors as Keating's Bar and Restaurant in December 2005. An important listed building, it boasts many outstanding features, such as Renatus Harris's organ and a spectacular stained-glass window.

LEFT: A street entertainer on Grafton Street.

DUBLIN

RIGHT: The Fusilier's Arch (referred to as the 'Traitors Gate' by some) forms the entrance to St. Stephen's Green at its Grafton Street corner and was erected in 1904. It commemorates the Royal Dublin Fusiliers who lost their lives during the Second Boer War.

FAR RIGHT: Leinster House, erected in 1745 for the Duke of Leinster to a design by Richard Cassels, is thought to have influenced the architecture of the White House in the U.S.A. It is here that both houses of the Irish Parliament (Oireachtas), the Dáil Éireann (lower house) and the Seanad Éireann (upper house) have met since 1924.

OPPOSITE: Dubliners and tourists relaxing in the central park of St. Stephen's Green.

DUBLIN

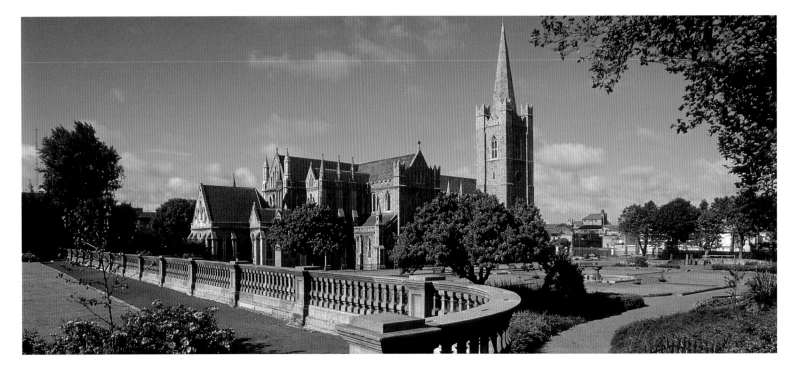

Dublin's St. Patrick's Cathedral, formally known as The National Cathedral and Collegiate Church of Saint Patrick, was founded in 1190. It is the larger of Dublin's two Church of Ireland cathedrals, and the largest church in Ireland. Unusually, it is not the seat of Dublin's Church of Ireland archbishop, whose seat is Christ Church Cathedral. Jonathan Swift, author of Gulliver's Travels, among many other satirical writings, was Dean of St. Patrick's between 1713 and 1745.

Among the treasures of Irish history in the National Museum are the many artefacts found on the Viking site at Wood Quay, from combs and brooches to swords and weighing-machines. The superb Tara Brooch and Ardagh Chalice, both dating from the eighth century, are in the museum's medieval collection, and there are other fine collections of Irish glass, lace and musical instruments, all imaginatively displayed.

A short walk from the museum is the National Gallery of Ireland, opened in 1864 and housing a comprehensive collection of paintings and sculpture covering most of the schools of European art; the gallery is also strong on Irish painting, including that of Jack B. Yeats, the brother of William Butler Yeats.

The National Library is of interest both for its fine collections of first editions and the works of Irish writers, also for the fact that James Joyce set Stephen Dedalus's literary debate in *Ulysses* in the library's Reading Room. To find the most famous books in Ireland, however – the *Book of Durrow* and the *Book of Kells* – it is necessary to visit the Old Library of Trinity College.

Trinity College, set in 40 secluded acres in the centre of Dublin, was founded by Elizabeth I in 1592 and is the only college making up Dublin University. The Long Room of Trinity's Old Library houses some 200,000 of the college's collection of over three million volumes, including the *Book of Kells*, a four-volume, superbly illuminated version of the Four Gospels. Two of the four volumes are usually on display in the library at any one time.

AWAY FROM THE CENTRE

Dublin has a fast and efficient commuter train service – the DART (Dublin Area Rapid Transport) – running around Dublin Bay and linking Howth to the north of the city with Bray, beyond Dún Laoghaire, to the south in County Wicklow. It is the ideal method of transportation to the area south of the city centre, beyond the Grand Canal, one of Dublin's two canals, and the suburbs of Crumlin, Rathmines and Donnybrook.

South of here is the area which has been called the Dubliners' playground. On the coast are attractive seaside villages, such as Blackrock, Sandycove, Dalkey (which can boast two castles, two harbours and a cottage in which George Bernard Shaw once lived), and Killiney, with its superb views across to Dalkey Island. Inland are the Dublin Mountains, with their forest walks and scenic drives, and other attractions include the racecourse at Leopardstown and the 40-acre (16-hectare) Fernhill Gardens lying south of Sandyford.

Trinity College, Dublin's university, was founded by Queen Elizabeth I in 1592. Today its lawns and cobbled quadrangles provide a haven of tranquillity at the heart of the city. Among many famous students to have attended the college were playwrights Oliver Goldsmith and Samuel Beckett.

Dún Laoghaire, on the southern curve of Dublin Bay, 9 miles (14km) south of Dublin, is both a major ferry terminal and the largest yachting centre in Ireland. The harbour, which has two mile-long piers, was built by the Scottish engineer, John Rennie, early in the 19th century. A short distance along the coast from Dún Laoghaire's harbour is Sandycove, a tiny village whose Martello tower accommodated James Joyce for a week in 1904, and on which the author bestowed literary immortality by setting the opening of *Ulysses* there. There is now a James Joyce Museum in the Martello tower, open in the summer months.

Like Dublin's city centre, Sandycove also celebrates Bloomsday on 16 June – the day in 1904 when all the events in *Ulysses* took place. For Joyce, Sandycove was as much a part of Dublin as the more famous streets and buildings in the centre of the city; when he said that after his death the word 'Dublin' would be found inscribed on his heart, he had the whole splendid spread of the city and its suburbs in his mind's eye.

OPPOSITE: Modern Dublin is represented by the International Financial Services Centre on the north bank of the Liffey adjacent to Custom House.

LEFT: An aerial view of Dalkey Island, lying a little way offshore from the attractive town of Dalkey, south of Dublin. As well as being a bird sanctuary, Dalkey Island also boasts a Martello Tower and Saint Begnet's Holy Well, reputed to cure rheumatism.

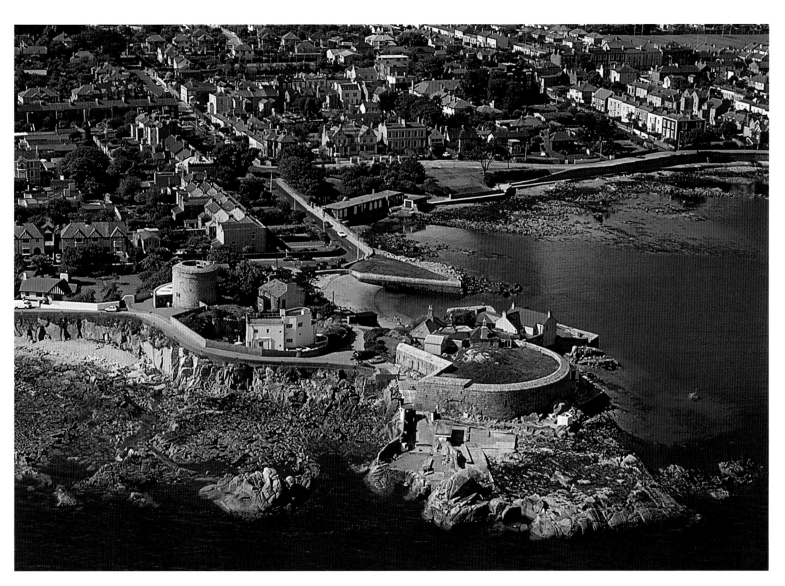

OPPOSITE: Children fishing from the harbour wall at Howth.

LEFT: Sandycove, at the southern end of Dublin Bay, is famous for its connections with James Joyce. Its Martello tower, the setting for the opening pages of Ulysses, *now houses a museum dedicated to the writer's life and work. The Forty Foot Pool, below the tower, also figures in the novel's early pages.*

PAGE 54: A fishing boat returning to Howth harbour. The island in the distance is known as Ireland's Eye.

PAGE 55: This other Martello tower, standing above the beach at Portmarnock, near Malahide, popular as a seaside resort for wealthy Dubliners in Georgian times, offered coastal defence during the Napoleonic Wars.

Oscar Wilde, photographed in New York in 1882, when he was known as a poet and an 'apostle of aesthetics'. The novel Dorian Gray *and the plays, including* Lady Windermere's Fan, An Ideal Husband *and* The Importance of Being Earnest, *which would bring him lasting fame, were not published until the 1890s.*

IRISH LITERATURE

Irish writers have contributed enormously to the body of literature written in English, and drama, poetry and fiction would be much the poorer but for the sparkling wit, rich vein of fantasy, and elegant satire executed in those particular and unique rhythms derived from Gaelic speech patterns and the Gaelic literary tradition. Ulster-born poet Seamus Heaney's Nobel Prize for Literature in 1995 was the fourth to be awarded to an Irish writer, the other three going to W.B. Yeats (1923), George Bernard Shaw (1925) and Samuel Beckett (1969).

At only a slightly less exalted level, writers from both the north and the south of Ireland have figured prominently in the lists of winners and short-listed contenders for the United Kingdom's Booker Prize for Fiction, among them the late Iris Murdoch (Dublin-born of Anglo-Irish parents), Roddy Doyle, Molly Keane and Brian Moore.

Molly Keane (1904–1996), following in the footsteps of Sheridan, Goldsmith, Wilde and Shaw, achieved early success in Britain as a playwright, using the name M.J. Farrell to conceal her identity, since well-brought-up Anglo-Irish girls did not write plays, let alone have them performed on the West End stage; by the time, many years later, that she began writing her brilliant and witty novels of life in the Anglo-Irish Big House, treading a path explored earlier in the century by Elizabeth Bowen, attitudes had radically changed and she was able to use her own name.

FAR LEFT: Celebrating Bloomsday, 16 June, has become part of the summer season in Dublin. This stylishly dressed couple stand beside the statue of James Joyce in North Earl St., sculpted by Marjorie Fitzgibbon.

LEFT: Bust of James Joyce, the creator of Leopold Bloom, on St. Stephen's Green.

DUBLIN

George Bernard Shaw at 70, by which time he had become the grand old man of Anglo-Irish literature. Born into an Irish Protestant family in Dublin in 1856, Shaw did most of his writing in England. Here he discovered Socialism, which became the driving force of his writing.

It was in the 17th century that many Irish writers began working in the English language rather than the Gaelic, which had been the language of the old Irish aristocracy, now deprived of its power and patronage. Now the Protestant Anglo-Irish were the ones wanting to

read poetry and stories and see new plays at the theatre, and they required them to be in English.

Even a satirist like Jonathan Swift, born in Dublin of English parents in 1667, who aimed his barbs in political satires, including Gulliver's Travels, *at the Anglo-Irish, knew that those same people would be a large part of his audience. Swift went on to become Dean of St. Patrick's Cathedral in Dublin, where he is buried and where several items of memorabilia associated with his name attract many visitors.*

A fellow student of Swift's at Trinity College, Dublin, was William Congreve; a few years after them, George Farquhar also studied there, the latter two becoming the leading playwrights of their day in England.

In fact, until well into the 20th century, most Irish writers wishing to achieve fame and fortune, or merely a modest living, had to leave Ireland to do so. After Congreve and Farquhar, the next Irish writers to set the London stage alight in the 18th century were Sheridan and Goldsmith. Late in the 19th century, the names had changed but the Irish talent was still very much in evidence with such luminaries as essayist George Moore and the playwrights Dion Boucicault, Oscar Wilde and George Bernard Shaw.

By now the Irish Revival, influenced by the Gaelic Revival at the end of the 19th century, had been gathering pace. The Abbey Theatre, backed by W.B. Yeats and Lady Gregory, produced its first play in 1904. Its subject, and that of the many plays which followed, including works by great writers like J.M. Synge and Sean O'Casey, was Ireland, Irish life and Irish history. They were not always well-received by Irish audiences quick to see immorality in word as well as in deed, and the first night of Synge's masterpiece, The Playboy of the Western World, *turned into a riot as a result of its 'immoral language'.*

While the Irish Revival meant that, from now on, many Irish writers, novelists and short-story writers, poets and dramatists would find as interested a market for their work at home as abroad, others, most notably James Joyce and Samuel Beckett, were forced to flee the narrowness of Irish society and seek sympathetic publishers abroad.

James Joyce, in particular, keenly felt the bitterness of exile from his beloved Dublin, the setting of his great works of fiction, including Dubliners, Portrait of the Artist as A Young Man *and* Ulysses. *It was not until the 1960s that* Ulysses, *till then perceived as pornographic, was taken off the Republic of Ireland's lengthy list of banned works. Today, Bloomsday, named after Leopold Bloom, a main character in* Ulysses *and celebrated on 16 June, the day on which the events of the novel take place, is a highlight of the summer season in and around Dublin.*

Patrick Kavanagh, the celebrated Irish poet, was in the habit of sitting beside Dublin's Grand Canal, where he contemplated his life and work. One of his poems is 'Lines Written on a Seat on the Grand Canal', so such a seat in this location seemed the ideal place for a statue of the poet, who died in 1967.

CHAPTER TWO
THE EASTERN COUNTIES

Louth, Meath, Dublin, Kildare, Wicklow

BELOW: The Mound of the Hostages on the Hill of Tara, a small passage grave holding mostly cremated Neolithic human remains.

OPPOSITE: The massive Anglo-Norman fortress of Trim Castle, dating from 1173, lies on a bank of the River Boyne.

The eastern counties of the Republic of Ireland – Louth, Meath, Kildare and Wicklow – that enclose Dublin in a crescent encompassing the coast of the Irish Sea to north and south – offer a splendid variety of scenery, from the quiet green pastures of Meath and Louth, touching the border with Northern Ireland in the north, to the rugged Wicklow Mountains in the south. Today, much of the region is fertile pastureland, the Bog of Allen in Kildare being the largest peatland area in Ireland, while the grassy plain of the Curragh,

Ireland's largest area of arable land, is the centre of the country's Thoroughbred racing industry.

Louth, a border county, and Meath, both of them once within the Pale, which was the boundary within which the English Crown had established total authority by about 1500, are areas of quiet farmland these days, attracting fewer holidaymakers and tourists than Wicklow or Kildare, also once within the Pale, despite the fine stretch of coast and numerous pleasant seaside resorts like Black Rock on Dundalk Bay and Bettystown, south of Drogheda.

County Meath, once part of an ancient province of Ireland ruled by the High Kings of Ireland from their palace crowning the Hill of Tara (south of Navan, Meath's county town), has more to show of its history than Louth. It is to Meath that anyone seriously interested in Ireland's past must come to discover the extraordinary megalithic tombs of the Boyne Valley; to trace the origins of Christianity in Ireland at such places as Kells and Monasterboice; to visit Trim Castle, the largest Anglo-Norman castle left in Ireland; and to walk down King William's Glen to the site of the Battle of the Boyne. Here, William III's defeat of the forces of James II in 1690 meant not only the end of the Catholic Stuart cause but also changed the balance of power in Europe, too.

Wicklow and Kildare, along with other parts of County Dublin beyond the limits of the capital's influence, have more

RIGHT: St. Patrick looks down on the Hill of Tara. For many centuries Tara was the seat of power for pagan priests and the High Kings of Ireland.

OPPOSITE LEFT: The round tower at Glendalough, part of the early monastery that was once regarded as among the finest seats of learning in Europe.

OPPOSITE RIGHT: An old anchor frames a view of the lighthouse at Howth harbour, a fishing port and yacht marina at the northern end of Dublin Bay. Before it silted up early in the 19th century, Howth was the main harbour for packet boats sailing between Ireland and England.

obvious attractions for visitors seeking to escape urban life. Wicklow, in particular, has many a fine refuge, both inland, where the peaks and valleys of the Wicklow Mountains make superb walking and mountain bike country, and where there are several beautiful houses and gardens to visit, including Powerscourt and Russborough House, both relics of Anglo-Irish life, and on the coast, where several seaside resorts of Victorian origin attract new generations of holidaymakers.

As mountains go, the Wicklows are little more than rounded, lowish to high hills (the highest peak, Lugnaquilla, is just over 3,000ft (915m) and only a few granite-covered peaks, such as Great Sugar Loaf Mountain, have resisted weathering to retain a jagged shape), but what they lack in terms of mountain grandeur is more than made up for in the quality of their uninhabited wildness. This was once bandit country, so it is hardly surprising that the only road cutting through the Wicklows, from north to south, was originally a military highway, built to prevent more uprisings, such as the Irish Rebellion of 1798, from occurring. The road still follows its original route, from Rathfarnham, in Dublin's southern suburbs, to Aghavannagh.

Part of the military road is also followed by the Wicklow Way, Ireland's first officially-designated long-distance walk. Also starting in Dublin's southern suburbs, the Wicklow Way follows an 82-mile (132-km) course to Clonegal on the Wexford border

in County Carlow, taking in some memorable locations such as Glencree, Lough Tay and Glendalough.

HISTORY ALONG RIVERS AND CANALS

The eastern counties are well provided with water, with several river systems as well as two of Ireland's fine canals within their limits. The canals, both of which are open to pleasure craft along sections, if not their whole lengths, are the Royal Canal and the Grand Canal. They were built in the 18th century, when Irish confidence in its country's trading future was at its height; both of them connect Dublin with the heart of Ireland on a parallel course north and south of the Liffey.

The Grand Canal, begun in 1756, was cut through Dublin south of the Liffey and had reached the Shannon by the early 19th century. It was used for freight until as recently as 1959. The Royal Canal, which also started in Dublin, but north of the Liffey, was cut through to Mullingar, reaching the Shannon by 1817. Both canals have been undergoing repair and renovation in recent years. Barge and waterbus trips are run on the Grand Canal at Robertstown, north of Kildare, and cruisers are available for hire at Tullamore. Monasterevin, west of Kildare, has a particularly fine aqueduct, which carries the Grand Canal over the River Barrow and attracts many canal enthusiasts.

Foremost among the rivers of the eastern counties are the Boyne, joined by the Blackwater at Navan before it flows down

the lovely fertile Boyne Valley; the Liffey, rising in the Wicklow Mountains and flowing through Kildare and into the Irish Sea at Dublin; the Barrow, which also waters part of Kildare on its southward journey to the Celtic Sea; and, in Wicklow, the Avoca, formed by the meeting of the rivers Avonmore and Avonbeg, and which reaches the sea at Arklow, a busy port and harbour town where shipbuilding has been important for several centuries: Sir Francis Chichester's famous *Gipsy Moth IV*, that he sailed around the world in 1966–67, was built in a yard here.

OPPOSITE: Ponies grazing in the Wicklows with Great Sugar Loaf Mountain in the background.

BELOW: A peaceful stretch of the Grand Canal at Mespil Road in Dublin. Built in the 18th century as a trading link with the River Shannon, it is now used for leisure activities.

To reach Arklow, the Avoca flows down a lovely valley, the Vale of Avoca, memorably described in Thomas Moore's poem, 'The Meeting of the Waters':

'There is not in this wide world a valley so sweet
As that vale in whose bosom the bright waters meet...'

It is a sentiment shared these days by the millions of viewers, in Britain and Ireland, of the popular television drama series, *Ballykissangel*, which was filmed in the picturesque village of Avoca at the heart of the Vale of Avoca. Handweaving has been one of the local trades for centuries, and the weavers of Avoca Mill, founded in 1723, are believed to have put in many extra hours of work to keep up with the demands of the stream of visitors that 'television tourism' tends to attract.

Because these rivers all reach the coast at accessible estuaries, it is not surprising they were used as a way into Ireland's heartland by Celts, Viking raiders and more peaceable Christian missionaries. Relics of their presence, from prehistoric passage graves and Viking hill forts to medieval monasteries, are to be found throughout the area.

The lovely Boyne Valley in County Meath, for instance, fertile and luxuriantly wooded, is just an hour's drive north of Dublin. Since time immemorial the river was a main route to the centre of Ireland from the coast, and Drogheda near its mouth was an important port; consequently the area is rich in prehistoric relics of the people who once inhabited the area and it could justifiably

OPPOSITE: A mountain road leads up from Laragh towards the Sally Gap in the Wicklow Hills.

LEFT: A weir on the River Boyne at Slane, County Meath.

RIGHT: The River Boyne below Oldbridge, where William III's army crossed to engage with that of James II in the 1690 Battle of the Boyne.

OPPOSITE: 'The Meeting of the Waters' in the Vale of Avoca was made famous by Thomas Moore's famous ballad.

RIGHT: A re-enactment of the Battle of the Boyne on the Oldbridge Estate, part of the battlefield near Drogheda.

OPPOSITE: Quiet fields by the River Boyne witnessed the clash of European armies, when over 60,000 men fought the Battle of the Boyne in 1690.

be called the cradle of Irish civilization. The great grave mounds, built on the north bank of the river along a stretch of the river between Tullyallen and Slane, called *Brú Na Bóinne,* 'Palace of the Boyne', and on hilltops facing towards the sun, still have the power to astonish and intrigue us today.

The prehistoric burial sites at Dowth, Knowth and Newgrange, completed by the time the ancient Egyptians began building their pyramids, are the oldest in the British Isles. Today, the most accessible to visitors is the passage tomb at Newgrange, which has been carefully restored and where visitors can follow a route, lined with standing stones, to a chamber where three recesses still hold the stone basins in which the bones of the dead, together with funeral offerings of stones and beads, were kept.

Kildare also has many relics of its ancient past, especially in the basin of the River Barrow. Among them is the hilltop fort at Knockaulin, where the great circular wall surrounding the fort,

OPPOSITE: Looking south-west over Lough Tay in the Wicklow Hills.

BELOW: The great prehistoric passage tomb of Newgrange, in the Boyne valley, was the scene of ritual burials over 5,000 years ago.

FAR RIGHT: In Newgrange's central chamber, deep inside the historic mound, can be found this Celtic triskelion symbol, carved into the stone.

BELOW RIGHT: The domed corbelled roof covering the central chamber.

OPPOSITE LEFT: The round tower at Donaghmore, County Meath, rises nearly 100ft (30m) on the medieval church site associated with St. Cassanus, a follower of St. Patrick.

OPPOSITE RIGHT: The 13th-century castle in ancient Ardee, Louth. Ardee is the site of the ford where the heroes Cúchullain and Ferdia fought a battle in the mythical epic of Táin Bó Cúailnge.

PAGE 76: The Abbey Church on the Hill of Slane in Meath, where St. Patrick lit a Paschal Fire in 433 in defiance of Tara's High King.

with a defensive ditch on the inside, is an important landmark. The site, first settled in the Stone Age, was a seat of the kings of Leinster, and was inhabited, so archeologists believe, until around AD 400.

Another centre of the kings of Leinster in Kildare is to be found on the wooded plain of the River Liffey. Naas, whose name translates as 'the castle of the Kings', is today the county town of Kildare, its commercial success built around the racing industry. Centuries ago, Naas, after the departure of the kings of Leinster, found itself a fortified town under Anglo-Norman rule. All that

remains of the rule of the kings is a mound called the North Motte, while Anglo-Norman remains of a 13th-century castle can be found in the grounds of the Protestant church of St. David. Perhaps more enjoyable for present-day visitors to Naas is the Canal Harbour, which was once a busy terminus with the Grand Canal and still has pleasant towpath walks.

CHRISTIANITY IN THE EASTERN COUNTIES

While the pre-Christian peoples of Ireland have left their mark on the landscape of the eastern counties, so too have those who brought Christianity to Ireland and established it as the religion of the country. Places like Kells, Monasterboice and Glendalough, whose names ring out strongly in the history of Christianity in Ireland, are all to be found in these parts, along with many relics of early Celtic Christianity, such as the high crosses at Old Kilcullen (said to be relics of a monastery founded here by St. Patrick himself), Castledermot and Moone in County Kildare, which also has, in Kildare town, a reminder of St. Brigid.

Brigid founded a monastery here in 490, on the site of which was built the Church of Ireland's Cathedral of St. Brigid at the end of the 12th century. The massive building seen in Kildare today, however, is a largely Victorian reconstruction, though its round tower is believed to date back to the original building.

Kells, famous for the magnificent four-volume manuscript of the Gospels, the *Book of Kells*, the illumination of which was either executed or completed there in the late eighth century, is

FAR LEFT: The crucifixion depicted on Muiredach's Cross at Monasterboice.

ABOVE: The ruins of Mellifont Abbey, the first Cistercian house to be founded in Ireland in 1142, stands beside the River Mattock, a subsidiary of the Boyne, in Louth.

RIGHT: Originally built in the sixth century, the 180-ft (55-m) Celtic Christian round tower stands beside St. Brigid's Cathedral, Kildare. It was rebuilt in the 12th century.

FAR RIGHT: A statue of St. Brigid holding the flame at St. Brigid's Holy Well, Kildare.

OPPOSITE: St. Brigid's Holy Well.

today a busy little market town in the valley of the Blackwater river in County Meath. The main relics of the monastery founded by St. Columba in the sixth century include a tenth-century much-weathered round tower, a stone cross, and a small stone oratory known as St. Columba's House. Its greatest treasure, the *Book of Kells*, has been in the library of Trinity College, Dublin, since the 17th century.

Monasterboice, also in County Meath, a few miles north of Drogheda, is the site of a monastery founded by St. Buithe (Boethius) in the early sixth century and is of particular interest among the monastic foundations of Ireland in that it was a dual foundation, for both men and women, and became an important seat of learning in later centuries. All that remains of the monastic site today are three splendid High Crosses, one of them 23ft (7m) high, carved with scenes from the Bible.

Two other Christian sites near Monasterboice are Mellifont and the Hill of Slane. Mellifont was Ireland's first Cistercian abbey, built beside the River Mattock by monks from France in the 12th century; enough of it remains to give a strong evocation of what the place must have been like in its heyday.

The Hill of Slane has been associated with Christianity in Ireland since its earliest days, for it was here that St. Patrick challenged the Druids, who were holding a pagan festival at Tara one Easter Eve. He should have been put to death, but he preached the gospel before the High King so eloquently that the

RIGHT: Stained glass showing St. Patrick and St. Columba in St. Brigid's Cathedral, Kildare.

FAR RIGHT: A sarcophagus cover, also from St. Brigid's Cathedral.

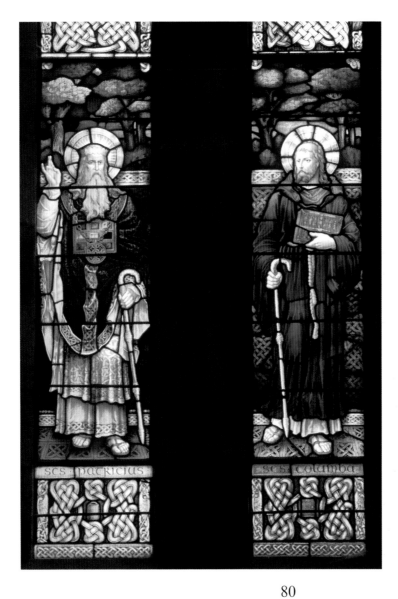

Intricate Celtic knotwork carved into the base of the Christian Celtic High Cross at Moone, Co. Kildare, that was constructed from granite during the eighth century. The theme of the cross, the second oldest in Ireland, is how God came to the assistance of individuals in their hour of need, and depicts Daniel in the lion's den, the three boys in the fiery furnace, and Jesus's miracle of the loaves and fishes. The monastery, dedicated to St. Columcille in the sixth century, is believed to have been founded by St. Palladius in the previous century.

BELOW: *Marlay House, built as a country manor house in the 18th century, is now in the southern Dublin suburb of Rathfarnham. Its grounds are now a public park.*

OPPOSITE: *Powerscourt, a Georgian demesne near Enniskerry, County Wicklow, with its Triton Lake and Italian Gardens.*

king allowed his subjects to choose for themselves between paganism and Christianity.

One of the most atmospheric of all Ireland's many Christian sites is in Wicklow, at Glendalough, the 'valley of the two lakes'. Here, in the sixth century, St. Kevin founded a monastery devoted to learning and the care of the sick which, after his death, became a place of pilgrimage. Despite being sacked several times by the Vikings, the monastery flourished for several centuries and was still active, though very much reduced, at the time of Henry VIII's

Dissolution of the Monasteries in the 16th century. Careful restoration of the site began in the 19th century and today Glendalough is an inspiring place to visit, with an excellent centre where visitors can be guided around the main points of interest and hear of the history of this very special place.

WITHIN THE PALE: HOUSES AND GARDENS

It was in the counties of the Pale in the 18th century that the Anglo-Irish felt most at home and most relaxed, ready to devote time and money to creating a domestic environment in which comfort and the enjoyment of the good things of life took precedence over thoughts of invasion and warfare, which had led Anglo-Normans to scatter the countryside with castles and towers.

Georgian-style architecture and building flourished in the eastern counties, leaving behind a splendid legacy of fine houses and gardens, whose pleasures can be enjoyed by many more people today than their builders ever imagined. While many impressive buildings dating from the heyday of Anglo-Irish society have, naturally enough, fallen into disrepair or disappeared altogether, many more are still inhabited as private residences, have been turned into fine country house hotels, or are among the most popular venues for Irish tourism.

An interesting example of house turned hotel is Kilkea Castle in County Kildare, a medieval stronghold of the

Fitzgeralds, which today's potential hotel guests may be relieved to know was much modernized and rebuilt in Victorian times. Today's owners of another Fitzgerald house, Carton House   at Maynooth, County Kildare, also have plans to turn this fine Georgian demesne into a hotel. It was once the country home of the 20th Earl of Kildare who, as Duke of Leinster, built the hugely grand Leinster House in Dublin, now the home of the two houses of the Irish Parliament.

The Earl of Kildare's wife was Lady Emily Lennox, whose sister Louisa married into the wealthy Conolly family, owners of Castletown House, also near Maynooth. Castletown and its attendant village, Celbridge, were intentionally designed and built on a grand scale to demonstrate the wealth of its owner, and much of the superbly designed and decorated interior was commissioned by Lady Louisa Conolly. Today, Castletown is in the care of the Irish Office of Public Works and is one of the most visited of Ireland's stately homes.

While County Kildare can also offer one of Ireland's most interesting gardens, the Japanese Gardens on the estate at Tully, which includes the Irish National Stud, it is in County Wicklow that Ireland's best-known house-and-garden estate, Powerscourt, is to be found. The house, originally a 13th-century castle, whose position was of strategic military importance in that it controlled access to the nearby Dargle, Glencree and Glencullen rivers, was extensively altered during the 18th century by

OPPOSITE: The view from Powerscourt, with the Great Sugar Loaf Mountain in the background.

LEFT: The bust of Leonardo da Vinci in Powerscourt's walled gardens, is a memorial to Julia, 7th Vicountess of Powerscourt.

PAGE 86: Detail of a wrought-iron gate in the walled gardens at Powerscourt.

PAGE 87: Powerscourt's impressive winged horses were cast in zinc by Professor Hugo Hagen in Berlin in 1869.

BELOW: St. Fiachra's Garden at the Irish National Stud at Tully.

OPPOSITE: The Japanese Garden, also at Tully, was the work of the Japanese Eida and his son Minoru.

German architect Richard Cassels, starting in 1731 and finishing ten years later. What was by now a once-splendid early 18th-century Palladian mansion was gutted by fire in 1974, the romantic ruin left to form a backdrop to part of the magnificent gardens, though it was not quite as splendid a setting as the dramatic peak of the Great Sugar Loaf Mountain which once dominated the house. Fortunately, Powerscourt was renovated in 1996, and today the estate is a popular tourist attraction, with a golf course, an Avoca Handweavers restaurant, and a Ritz-Carlton hotel.

Not far from Powerscourt is Killruddery House, lying in the shadow of Little Sugar Loaf Mountain near Bray. Built in the mid-17th century, Killruddery is the seat of the earls of Meath and is today mainly visited for its superb gardens, complete with ponds, canals and a sylvan theatre, designed in formal French Classical style and laid out by a French gardener who once worked at Versailles.

It is not the gardens that take people to Russborough House, also in County Wicklow, near Blessington, so much as the magnificent collection of paintings exhibited there. The collection was the work of the 19th-century entrepreneur, Alfred Beit, a co-founder of the De Beer Diamond Mining Company in South Africa. He left the collection, including works by Rubens, Frans Hals, Velazquez, Murillo, Goya and Gainsborough, to his nephew, Sir Alfred Beit, who chose to house them in the splendidly decorated Palladian mansion, Russborough House, which he bought in 1952.

Today, such houses seem to need more protection than they did in the 18th century, for Russborough has been burgled twice, once by a woman attempting to raise funds for the IRA, and once by international art thieves. Bridget Rose Dugdale's haul was found on a farm in County Cork, but only a fraction of that taken during the second break-in has been found – in the Netherlands.

ARCHITECTURE IN IRELAND

A wealth of building styles are to be discovered in Ireland, despite the actions of invading hordes throughout the centuries – Vikings, Anglo-Normans, Cromwell's army, the Black and Tans in the south, the IRA in the north, even present-day 'developers' – who have all cut destructive swathes through the island's architectural heritage.

While much of Ireland's domestic architecture remains, as the description implies, in the form of houses in which people actually lived, there is a great deal that has been carefully preserved or restored and is open to the general public. Visitors can discover for themselves, scattered the length and breadth of the country, the realities of life in Stone Age forts and Bronze Age crannogs, early Christian monasteries, Anglo-Norman castles, fine Georgian country houses, and tiny one-roomed cottages.

The entire spectrum of pre-Christian Ireland is laid before us in the remains of burial sites, including tombs, dolmens and cemeteries, and in several splendid Iron Age forts. There are also two excellent reconstructions of prehistoric buildings at Craggaunowen in County Clare and at the Ulster History Park, a splendid open-air museum in County Tyrone.

Particularly impressive are the dolmens or portal tombs dating from the megalithic period, including the Browne's Hill Dolmen in County Carlow, which still supports the biggest capstone in Ireland, weighing in at about 100 tons, and the Legananny Dolmen in the Mountains of Mourne in County Down. Just about the most

OPPOSITE: Hook Head Lighthouse, at the southern tip of the Hook Head Peninsula, marks the eastern side of Waterford harbour; the site of the oldest lighthouse in Europe and one of the oldest in the world. The first light was a beacon, lit here by monks in the fifth century.

LEFT: The raised ridges and trenches of the adjacent ancient earthworks known as Cormac's House and the Royal Seat on the Hill of Tara.

important Stone Age passage tomb in Europe can be found at Newgrange in Meath, standing in a great area of ancient tombs known as Brú Na Bóinne.

The best places to see the remains of entire Stone Age settlements are at Lough Gur in Limerick and Céide Fields in County Mayo. Much of the latter site was buried and preserved under bog and archeologists have been able to uncover enough of the remains of stone walls and farm buildings to indicate that a sizeable community once lived and farmed in the vicinity.

As for Stone Age ring forts, one of the best preserved is Staigue Fort on the Iveragh peninsula in Kerry, while the Iron Age forts on the Hill of Tara, visible only as hollows and grassy mounds, remain deeply evocative of Celtic Ireland.

The earliest Christians in Ireland left few remains because their settlements were built of perishable wattle and daub and their churches, some of them reputed to be very fine indeed, were made of wood. Later, they began to raise impressive stone crosses, magnificently carved, and many of these survive, notably at Monasterboice in County Louth, Clonmacnoise in Offaly, and Kells in Meath.

The earliest stone churches, most of them with thatched roofs, were single-chambered, with a west door and small east window; a particularly fine example of a rare stone-roofed single-chamber church is the Gallarus Oratory on the Dingle peninsula in County Kerry.

With marauding Vikings on the rampage throughout the land, people living in and around Christian monasteries began to build slender, tapering round towers of stone. Some were intended as bell towers, but many were seen as places of refuge and for storing precious manuscripts. Often the entrances were high up above ground level, accessible by ladders which could be hauled back up into the tower when the need arose.

About 70 round towers still survive in Ireland today, many of them in a surprisingly good state of repair, the perfectly preserved 82-ft (25-m) tower on Devenish Island in County Fermanagh, the even taller tower by the ruins of the Romanesque-style St. Declan's Cathedral at Ardmore in Waterford, and the Temple Finghin tower at Clonmacnoise monastery in Offaly being three such examples. The round tower at Timahoe in County Laois, rising 100ft (30m) above the village and a wood notable for its noisy colony of rooks, is famous for the elaborate carvings around its entrance arch, which is set 16ft (5m) above the ground.

There is also a round tower among the many monastic buildings at Glendalough in Wicklow in a particularly atmospheric Christian settlement begun by St. Kevin in the sixth century; this functioned as such right up to Henry VIII's Dissolution of the Monasteries in the 16th century.

The round towers of the Celtic Christians were built between the 10th and 12th centuries and by the end of this period the Anglo-Normans were moving into Ireland in increasing numbers,

OPPOSITE: The round tower is a familiar architectural feature in Ireland. This example is near Omeath on the Cooley peninsula, looking south from the top of Carlingford, County Louth.

their castles beginning to appear throughout the countryside. The earliest castles in Ireland were of the Norman motte-and-bailey type, involving a wooden tower on a raised mound surrounded by a ditch, so familiar to the Anglo-Saxons in England. Later, the Anglo-Normans began to erect much more formidable square stone keeps, which grew into mighty castles such as those at Trim and Carrickfergus.

Then, in 1429, Henry VI offered a £10 subsidy for anyone constructing a castle of a given minimum size in Ireland. Thus began the period of the tower house, more fortified residence than castle, examples of which were built all over Ireland between the 15th and 17th centuries. Among the most visited of these today are Bunratty Castle in Clare and Blarney Castle in County Cork. Thoor Ballylee, near Gort in County Galway, is famous as W.B. Yeats's summer home for most of the 1920s.

The 18th century was a period of relative stability and a quiet time for Ireland, during which the ruling Anglo-Irish no longer felt the need for fortified houses. They began to build country mansions in Palladian or neo-Classical style instead, some of which were constructed around existing castles: but many of them were designed from scratch by such architects as Richard Cassels (later Castle) and James Wyatt, most of them surrounded by walled gardens and parks, where a gracious, comfortable lifestyle could be maintained in surroundings of often considerable luxury.

Today, the style and grandeur of these great houses can be best appreciated by visits to Mount Stewart in County Down, Malahide Castle in County Dublin, Rowallane in County Down (headquarters of the National Trust in Northern Ireland), Bantry House (overlooking Bantry Bay in County Cork), and splendid properties like Powerscourt, Castletown House and Russborough House – all built within reach of Dublin at a time when it was the centre of the Anglo-Irish world.

OPPOSITE: Holding the much coveted farmlands of Kilkenny necessitated the construction of defensive walls and towers around Kells Priory.

BELOW: One of the finest possessions of the National Trust in Northern Ireland, Mount Stewart, near Newtownards in County Down, is a fine 18th-century mansion and gardens.

CHAPTER THREE

THE SOUTH & SOUTH-EAST

Wexford, Waterford, Carlow, Kilkenny, Tipperary

RIGHT: Reginald's Tower, part of Waterford's city walls, which were originally built by the Vikings and greatly extended by King John in the 12th century, has rececntly been restored to give today's visitors a glimpse of its medieval originals.

OPPOSITE: St. Mary's Abbey in Ferns dates from 1160. Now a small village in County Wexford, Ferns was once a royal episcopal city and an ancient capital of the province of Leinster.

The original Gaelic name for Ireland's south-eastern corner is *Cuan-na-groith*, 'haven of the sun', and it is well-deserved. This region of fine river valleys, fertile agricultural land – perhaps at its finest in the Golden Vale in Tipperary – and scenic hill country, with a coast lapped by the warm waters of the Gulf Stream, boasts the highest hours-of-sunshine count in Ireland.

It also has some of the loveliest beaches in the country, several of them fringing popular holiday resorts on the east coast. There is good walking country for the more energetic all over the region, in the Galtee Mountains in Tipperary, the Knockmealdowns in Waterford, the South Leinster Way in Carlow, Kilkenny and Tipperary, the Munster Way between Carrick-on-Suir and Clonmel, and the southern section of the Wicklow Way in County Carlow. Little wonder, then, that the region still experiences great invasions every year, though now, instead of Vikings and Anglo-Normans, the incomers are holidaymakers, both from home and abroad, with Rosslare harbour, a major port for ferries from Wales and France, being the first sight of Ireland for many of them.

Centuries ago, the majority of Viking and Anglo-Norman invaders of Ireland, as well as at least one Christian missionary before them, also had their first glimpse of the country from the St. George's Channel and the Celtic Sea. They chose to come this way because the natural harbours and river estuaries of the south-eastern coast offered, via several fine river valleys, direct routes into the heartland of Ireland.

The Vikings found a land with few towns (the Celts were herders of cattle and growers of crops rather than town-dwellers) but with a well-established network of Christian monasteries. St. Declan is reputed to have first set foot in Ireland at Ardmore in County Waterford a generation before St. Patrick returned from France in 432. At that time, control of the countryside was in the hands of the Celtic kings and although the Vikings destroyed many monastic and other religious foundations, many more survived. Outstanding among these were the monastery and chapel built on the great limestone outcrop, the Rock of Cashel, on the Tipperary plain, which was also the seat of the kings of Munster and is today one of the important relics of the early Christian period in Ireland.

Three of the five present-day counties in the region, Wexford, Carlow and Kilkenny, were at one time part of the ancient province of Leinster, whereas Waterford, while also a part of Leinster at one time, was for most of the period of the kings of Ireland part of Munster, along with Tipperary.

It was a 13th-century king of Leinster, Dermot MacMurrough, who 'invited' the Anglo-Normans into Ireland. Richard FitzGilbert de Clare, Earl of Pembroke, widely known as Strongbow, entered Ireland in 1170 by way of Waterford harbour, into which flow three of the great rivers of the south-east, the Nore, the Barrow and the Suir. Further east, the Slaney, flowing into Wexford harbour, begins its journey to the sea far to the north in the Wicklow Mountains – another way into the heartland for any raider arriving on Ireland's southern shores.

Strongbow beseiged Waterford, a Viking town of some size and importance, for three days before overcoming it. He then consolidated his position by marrying King Dermot's daughter, Aoife. Their marriage was celebrated in Reginald's Tower, built in Waterford by the Viking chief Ragnvald (or Reginald) the Dane at the beginning of the 11th century. The tower, having survived an attempt by Cromwell to capture it, has in its time been a mint, a prison and an army barracks; today it is a showpiece of Waterford's tourist industry, and is the town's Civic Museum.

OPPOSITE: The evening sunlight gives a golden glow to the roofs and steeples of the city of Wexford and to the waters of the Slaney.

FAR LEFT: Wexford's 1798 Memorial recalls the support for the Rising of the United Irishmen who sought to end British rule in Ireland. County Wexford was the centre of the 1798 rebellion, and Wexford city was held by the rebels throughout the fighting. It was the scene of a notorious massacre of local loyalists by the United Irishmen, who executed them on the bridge in the centre of Wexford city.

LEFT: Regarded as Ireland's national bard, it is not uncommon for the poet and balladeer Thomas Moore, whose mother was a Wexford girl, to be saluted with a few pints.

THE VIKINGS IN THE SOUTH-EAST

Scattered across the region, much of which is fertile agricultural country today, are a few reminders of its Viking past and a great many of its Anglo-Norman heritage. Although the ridge of granite of the Wicklow and Blackstair Mountains tended to present a natural barrier in prehistoric times between the people living on the fertile plain, between mountain and sea, and those living beyond the mountains in Carlow and Kilkenny, the existence of several rivers, carving fine valleys through the mountains and across the plains, meant that the Vikings, arriving in their longboats from Norway and Denmark early in the eighth century, were able to penetrate far inland from the island's south-eastern coast.

The two main coastal towns here, Wexford and Waterford, like Arklow and Wicklow further north, were both important Viking trading posts. Wexford's Viking name, *Waesfjord*, means 'the harbour of the mudflats' and Waterford's *Vadrefjord* means, appropriately enough, 'weather haven'. Both Wexford and Waterford still show, in the pattern of their narrow streets, strong signs of the centuries of Viking occupation. Waterford, now more famous for its fine crystal than its past history, is still able to show visitors not only Reginald's Tower, but also several fragments of the fortified wall the Vikings built after their arrival here in the ninth century.

While Wexford town retains very few relics of its ancient past, and owes its regular 'invasion' as much to visitors to its famous

international Wexford Opera Festival as to its history, the county has managed to recreate its past at the excellent Irish National Heritage Park, built at Ferrycraig, a few miles up the Slaney from Wexford harbour. Here, visitors can experience daily life in ancient Ireland, including a reconstruction of a Viking settlement, complete with thatched roundhouses made of mud, straw and animal skins, set behind palisades of wood and straw. A Viking longboat is moored nearby on the Slaney, the longest of the rivers flowing into the sea at Wexford.

Viking raiders left their mark much further inland, too. A grim reminder of the effects of a Viking raid recently came to light in the Dunmore Cave, situated in the limestone country north of Kilkenny, which has a good share of Irish myth and legend attached to its many caverns and stalactite-hung galleries. The bones of 50 people, mostly women and children and dating from the early tenth century, were found in the cave in 1973. The fact that none of the skeletons had broken bones suggests the people were taking refuge from a Viking raid, only to die of starvation or, in the event of an attempt having been made to smoke them out, suffocation.

THE ANGLO-NORMAN HERITAGE

If the Vikings left few obvious signs of their presence in this part of Ireland, the Anglo-Normans left a great many, often buildings on land given them by the Crown, partly as a means of

OPPOSITE: Hook Lighthouse, that guards to way to Waterford harbour, is a unique example of an almost intact medieval lighthouse. It dates from the early 13th century and was a major feat of engineering at the time of its construction.

LEFT: The Irish National Heritage Park at Ferrycraig, situated beside the River Slaney in County Wexford, contains a collection of recreated settlements spanning the period from 7000 BC to the arrival of the Normans in the 12th century.

OPPOSITE: The renovated castle at the centre of the lively town of Enniscorthy at the highest navigable point of the River Slaney in County Wexford.

LEFT: The harvest has been completed on this farm below the Blackstairs Mountains near the village of Borrisin in County Carlow.

PAGE 104: The Clashganna Lock on the River Barrow, with County Kilkenny on its western bank and County Carlow to the east.

PAGE 105: The rich farmland of County Carlow, near Tullow, looking south to the Blackstairs Mountains.

controlling the country. Great castle-builders, the Anglo-Normans were also strong supporters of the church – though they never hesitated to destroy any monastery whose occupants failed to toe the Anglo-Norman line – and in many places castles and monasteries, with their attendant places of worship, existed virtually side by side.

From Cahir (also spelt Caher) in County Tipperary to Enniscorthy in Wexford, and from Dungarven and Lismore in County Waterford to Kilkenny, ancient castles, some in ruins, some restored, and some with more modern buildings on their medieval foundations, still have plenty to tell us about the Anglo-Normans and their successors. One or two do not, however: Carlow, well-sited on the River Barrow and therefore of strategic importance, was once dominated by a massive early 13th-century pile. All that is left of it today, hidden in the grounds of a mineral-water factory, are a couple of towers and a fragment of wall. Far from being one of the many 'ruins that Cromwell knocked about a bit', to quote Marie Lloyd's song, Carlow's castle survived to the 19th century in good enough condition for a local doctor to consider turning it into a mental hospital. Unfortunately, in a praiseworthy attempt to get as much fresh air as possible into his castle hospital, he chose to use gunpowder to enlarge the windows in the thick walls and succeeded in reducing most of the castle to a pile of rubble.

Although little remains of Carlow Castle, there are many others with much to attract visitors. Cahir Castle and Ormond

BELOW RIGHT: Most of Lismore Castle, built by King John above the Blackwater in County Waterford in 1185, was rebuilt in the 19th century.

OPPOSITE: Lismore has an interesting history dating from the days of St.Carthagh, who founded a monastery and important seat of learning here in the seventh century.

PAGE 108: The Barrow and Suir rivers reach the sea here at Waterford, having been channels of commerce and invasion since the time of the Vikings.

PAGE 109: Old buildings on the River Suir, which flows through Waterford and is the reason for its long maritime history..

Castle at Carrick-on-Suir, both in County Tipperary, look fine enough to be film sets, Cahir with its square keep and crenellated walls on a rock in the middle of the Suir, and Ormond Castle, in contrast, all gabled and mullioned as befits a building often called 'the finest Elizabethan manor house in Ireland'.

Down in County Waterford, Lismore Castle, originally built, like Dungarvan Castle, at the handsome port of Dunvargan for Henry II's son John (the King John of Magna Carta fame) offers yet another view of Irish castles. Set proudly on a cliff above the Blackwater, Lismore is not all it appears to be. In the

OPPOSITE: The medieval cathedral, round tower and Cormac's Chapel, consecrated in 1134, sit on the Rock of Cashel in Tipperary, reputed to be the site of the conversion of the King of Munster by St. Patrick in the fifth century.

LEFT: Looking north over farmland towards Cahir from Sugarloasf Hill, a peak in the Knockmealdown Mountains that are situated on the border between Counties Tipperary and Waterford.

OPPOSITE: The ruins of Athassel Abbey, the Augustinian Priory of St. Edward the King, located on the western bank of the River Suir 5 miles (8km) south-west of Cashel, County Tipperary.

LEFT: A 'soft' day in County Tipperary, looking south across the lush Glen of Aherlow to the Galtee Mountains.

PAGE 114: The Old Mill on the River Nore at Bennettsbridge in County Kilkenny houses the pottery of Nicholas Mosse, one of Ireland's many excellent potteries, producing attractive spongeware ceramics that are famous throughout the world.

PAGE 115: Arable farmland near Kells, County Kilkenny, bathed in the last vestiges of evening light.

19th century its owner, the sixth Duke of Devonshire, brought in his old friend, Joseph Paxton, builder of the Crystal Palace (as well as additions to the duke's ancestral pile, Chatsworth in Derbyshire) to rebuild Lismore Castle. Today the castle, still owned by the Devonshires, is of interest because of its superb gardens, where the Elizabethan poet, Edmund Spenser, is thought to have composed part of *The Faerie Queene*.

Spenser also had connections with Enniscorthy Castle in Wexford (page 102), which was briefly leased to him by Queen Elizabeth I, so flattered was she by his great poem. Enniscorthy Castle today houses the County Wexford Historical and Folk Museum but, for many people, the castle holds something much more intangible than mere museum relics. The final, and bloodiest, struggle of the 1798 Rebellion was fought almost at the castle's feet, on Vinegar Hill, where the rebels held out for a month. The castle preserves many relics of the battle, and perhaps something of its atmosphere, too: local people say that if you climb Vinegar Hill of a summer's evening and stand by the windmill where the rebels made their last stand, the sounds of the battle can be clearly heard.

Although Enniscorthy has had a castle since the 12th century and Christian connections for much longer, St. Senan having founded a monastic settlement here in the sixth century, it can no longer show the sort of living connection between medieval church and Norman castle which makes Kilkenny, for instance, so interesting.

OPPOSITE & PAGE 118:
Thoroughbred brood mares with their foals at the Irish National Stud at Tully, near Kildare, the centre of Irish horse racing.

PAGE 119: They're off! The beginning of another race at one of Ireland's 25 racetracks.

AROUND KILKENNY

Virtually the capital of Ireland in the mid-17th century, the county town of Kilkenny is the most outstanding medieval town in Ireland, its centre dominated by St. Canice's Cathedral, named after the saint who founded a monastery here in the sixth century, and Kilkenny Castle, built by Strongbow's son-in-law, William, Earl of Pembroke, between 1192 and 1207 on a site dominating the River Nore and the surrounding countryside. The two mighty buildings are linked by a centuries-old street pattern formed by narrow alleyways of obviously medieval origin. There are many historic gems, ranging from Black Abbey, the medieval church of a Franciscan friary, to the 14th-century Kyteler's Inn and the Elizabethan Rothe House, now Kilkenny's local museum.

While Kilkenny carefully preserves its medieval past, to the delight of thousands of visitors every year, it also fosters a fine artistic tradition, and the Kilkenny Arts Festival, held each August, is now one of the most important in Ireland.

Most visitors to Kilkenny also find time to visit the monastic sites in the Nore valley. The ruins of Kells Priory, founded by Augustinian friars from Bodmin in Cornwall and later rebuilt behind a strongly fortified enclosure, are extensive, as are the ruins of the Cistercian Jerpoint Abbey, near Thomastown, another once-fortified medieval settlement. Jerpoint Abbey still has among its ruins the effigies of two bishops and, in its fine cloisters, many remarkable carvings, the details of which give fascinating glimpses into the medieval past of this part of Ireland.

THE IRISH AND THEIR HORSES

The internal combustion engine may long since have seen off the horse as a main means of transport in Ireland, as everywhere else, but in Ireland, particularly, the horse remains an essential pre-occupation of Irish life and society. The reasons are partly historical and partly a natural phenomenon.

Stone Age farmers are thought to have been the first to introduce the horse to Ireland about 4,000 years ago, while Celtic invaders introduced horse-drawn chariots much later on. At the end of the 16th century, Spanish Arabian horses, washed ashore from the ships of the Armada wrecked on Ireland's western coasts, are thought to have interbred with the native Connemara ponies, producing a horse of surpassing hardiness and speed.

The sturdy Connemara pony, along with the Irish Draught, which gives Irish showjumpers, eventers and hunters their strength and great jumping ability, are among nature's reasons for the pre-eminence of the horse in Irish life. Others are the mild climate and the country's underlying limestone foundation, which provides the soil with the calcium and minerals essential for building strong bones. Then, of course, there is that indefinable extra, the affinity between man and horse, which seems infinitely stronger in Ireland than elsewhere.

A CELEBRATION OF IRELAND

Early in the 1990s an official count revealed that there were about 55,000 horses in Ireland, of which nearly a quarter were racehorses. Racing horses has been part of the fabric of life in Ireland for centuries and kings, both legendary and historic, had their private racing greens. Horse fairs and public assemblies gave ordinary folk the chance to take part in racing, too, although a ban by Oliver Cromwell on Sunday racing, followed by the upheavals in Irish life after the Battle of the Boyne, put a distinct dampener on racing. Steeplechasing began quietly to fill the gap and by the mid-18th century was well-established in Ireland, with hundreds of race meetings taking place all over the country. The first race officially to be called a steeplechase took place in 1752, when two men raced each other between Buttevant and Doneraile in County Cork, using the spire of St. Leger Church in Doneraile as a guide to their finishing post.

Today there is virtually year-round racing at some 280 meetings in Ireland, whether racing on the flat, National Hunt racing, or point-to-point. Irish horses, moreover, are often to be seen grabbing attention in racing outside Ireland, particularly in England, where an Irish horse first won the Grand National in 1880 and the Derby some 20 years later. Needless to say, Ireland has its own Grand National and Derby, both of which were first run in the 19th century.

Among the highlights of the Irish racing calendar are the National Festival of Steeplechasing at Punchestown, 20 miles (32km) from Dublin, in April; the Irish Grand National, run on Easter Monday at Fairyhouse in County Meath; the Irish Derby at the

OPPOSITE: The horse fair at Spancil Hill, near Ennis in County Clare, has been held in June every year since the charter was first granted in the 17th century.

Curragh, County Kildare, in June/July; and the uniquely Irish Laytown races, run on the beach at Laytown, south of the Boyne estuary, in July or August, depending on the state of the tide. Then there is a whole string of important race meetings during the year at Leopardstown, a racecourse in Dublin's southern suburbs, and at three summer festivals of racing in County Kerry, at Killarney, Tralee and Listowel.

The Thoroughbred industry in Ireland is centred on the Curragh, a grassy plain in County Kildare, where many of the country's studs and training yards are situated. The Irish National Stud was established at Tully on the western edge of the Curragh in 1945, its main aim being the improvement of the quality of bloodstock in Ireland. The stud had been formed in 1900 by an eccentric Anglo-Irish breeder, Lord Wavertree, who, believing in the powers of astrology, had skylights installed in the stables to ensure that the power of the moon and stars would be transferred to his horses.

Today, parts of the stud are open to visitors, and there is a museum where, among other things, can be seen the skeleton of the great Irish steeplechaser, Arkle, which won England's Cheltenham Gold Cup three times in a row in the 1960s; and it must not be forgotten that Red Rum, another three-times winner of a great English steeplechase, the Grand National, was also Irish-bred.

For all enthusiasts of equestrianism, whatever their favoured discipline, the social highlight of the year is the Dublin Horse Show

in August, which attracts contestants, particularly to showjumping, and spectators from all over the world. Many of the horses competing here will have been purchased at Ireland's bloodstock sales, the most important of which are at Kill, County Kildare, or at the main national hunt sales, Tattersalls, at Fairyhouse in County Meath.

To the average horse-lover, however, the best and most enjoyable events are the traditional non-Thoroughbred fairs which have been part of Irish life for centuries. The oldest and most famous of these in Ireland, and once one of the three greatest horse fairs in Europe, is Galway's Great October Fair, held at Ballinasloe. Back in the 18th century, agents of the great powers of Europe came to Ballinasloe to buy cavalry horses – including, so tradition has it, Napoleon's horse Marengo (though this is denied by those who run the July horse fair at Cahirmee in County Cork, which also claims to have supplied Napoleon with his famous steed). Today, the Great October Fair is a lively occasion, offering thousands of visitors horse racing and street entertainment as well as the horse sales.

CHAPTER FOUR
THE MIDLANDS

Monaghan, Cavan, Longford, Westmeath, Offaly, Laois

The two most prominent architectural features of Athlone, Westmeath, are the 19th-century Church of Saints Peter and Paul and the 13th-century castle, set in close proximity to each other on the west bank of the River Shannon.

The Hill of Uisneach, between Mullingar and Athlone in County Westmeath, is considered, at least by local people, to be at the geographical centre of Ireland (people living further south near Birr in County Offaly also make the same claim). The famous Catstone on the Hill of Uisneach once marked the point of intersection between the five great provinces (or kingdoms) of ancient Ireland, Connacht, Munster, Leinster, Meath and Ulster.

OPPOSITE RIGHT & LEFT:
Irish Whiskey is almost as popular as Scotch. This is Locke's Distillery, situated in the town of Kilbeggan, Westmeath.

PAGE 124: Cloghan Castle, just outside the pleasant little town of Banagher, County Offaly, where the young Anthony Trollope worked as a surveyor for the Post Office, has been inhabited without interruption for 800 years.

PAGE 125: Pleasure boats moored on the Shannon at Clondra in County Longford. Clondra is an attractive village about 5 miles (8km) west of Longford and marks the end of the Royal Canal where it reaches the River Shannon.

Present-day Monaghan and Cavan, along with Donegal further west, are the only counties of the old province of Ulster not to have been included in the new Province of Northern Ireland at the time of Partition.

Stand on the flat top of this not particularly high hill, which is 620ft (190m) at its highest point, and you can certainly see much of these ancient provinces: on a clear day, it is said that the O'Connell Monument in Dublin's Glasnevin Cemetery, more than 90 miles (145km) away, can be seen, although much of the view is of farmland and quiet, green tranquillity.

The country of these six Midland counties is characterized by grassland and peatland, or raised bog country (as distinct from the blanket bog of the west of Ireland), especially in County Offaly, set between Boora Bog in the west and the Bog of Allen in the east. It is dotted with many loughs, while part of the borderland between Laois and Offaly is fine hill country, popular with walkers and hikers, the main range of which comprises the Slieve Bloom Mountains. Legend tells that these were formed when the music of a west Laois piper caused the trees and rocks to jig vigorously up and down.

Although the mountains are not very high, the highest point, Alderin, reaching only 1,735ft (530m), the country is rugged and desolate enough to give a real feeling of a wilderness. Try walking the 20-mile (32-km) circular Slieve Bloom Way, one of a couple of dozen well-signposted walks in the mountains, and you will

BELOW: The Shannon-Erne Waterway near Ballinamore. The waterway links upper Lough Erne in County Fermanagh and the River Shannon at Leitrim, following the channel of a canal which fell into disuse in the mid-19th century and which was repaired and re-opened in 1993.

encounter woods, moorland and bog, trace a section of one of the old high roads to Tara, and follow the bed of a pre-Ice Age river valley. If you are lucky, you may also see such wildlife as the Irish hare, the rare pine marten, fallow deer, and even mountain goats, as well as many species of birdlife.

Hill country of a different kind, being the small, rounded hills known as drumlins, shaped by the ice and glaciers of the last great Ice Age, is a characteristic of Cavan and Monaghan. Many

The reedy shores of Lough Ree, County Longford, one of three major lakes on the River Shannon. Lough Ree is the second largest lake on the Shannon after Lough Derg.

BELOW: Detail of the façade of Longford's St. Mel's Roman Catholic Cathedral, built of grey limestone in the 19th century.

OPPOSITE: Lea Castle in Laois.

of these drumlins show signs of prehistoric inhabitation, for the tops of hills were good places on which to build fortified settlements, and the remains of countless ancient tombs and ring forts are dotted over them, most of which have been left undisturbed for centuries.

COUNTRY OF RIVERS AND LOUGHS

Many of the people responsible for building these settlements were able to penetrate the interior of Ireland by means of its rivers and streams, for this is a region of many waterways, loughs and canals.

The two great canals of the region are the Royal Canal, cutting west across Westmeath and Longford from Dublin to reach the Shannon upriver of Lough Ree, and the Grand Canal, also coming out of Dublin, but further south through Offaly. The Royal Canal has been undergoing major restoration work in recent years, and has some pleasant towpath walks along its banks, from places like Ballymahon and around Mullingar, Westmeath's county town, which the Royal Canal almost encircles. The Grand Canal is well supplied with companies hiring out pleasure cruisers and narrowboats from many of the towns and villages along its course, and one of them, Tullamore, the county town of Offaly, actually owed much of its 19th-century prosperity to the Grand Canal, which reached the town in 1798.

In County Cavan, a third great canal system has taken shape in recent years. This is the realization of an old dream to link the Shannon and Erne rivers with a canal and thus create a major waterway system in the Midlands. The scheme is centred on Ballyconnell in north-western Cavan, where the Woodford river is a link in the scheme, and Ballinamore in County Leitrim. The Shannon-Erne Waterway has been open since 1993, providing a

system of rivers and linking canals to transport waterborne holidaymakers through Cavan.

Cavan, in which the two great rivers, the Shannon and the Erne, both have their sources, is said to have as many loughs as there are days in the year. Much of the heart of Westmeath is dotted with loughs, including Sheelin (shared with County Cavan), Lene, Derravaragh, Owel and Ennell. Many of these are familiar names in Irish folklore: Lough Derravaragh, for instance, is said to have been the home for 300 years of the children of the King of Lir, turned into swans by their jealous stepmother. Today, it is not folklore so much as the fine fishing in the lough, as well as the splendours of nearby Tullynally Castle, home to ten generations of the Pakenham family, earls of Longford, which attract visitors to the area.

County Longford, bordered in the west by the Shannon, also has numerous loughs which, though they may be of little interest to the average tourist, attract many anglers and watersports enthusiasts, as do rivers like the Inny, well-known for its coarse fishing and its trout.

One of the largest loughs of the Midlands is Lough Ree, where the borders of Longford, Westmeath and Offaly meet. The River Inny, flowing into Lough Ree south-west of Ballymahon, a town with many associations with Oliver Goldsmith, is just one of many attractive waterways in the region. Also notable in and on the shores of Lough Ree is Inchcleraun, an island whose six

OPPOSITE: Clonmacnoise in County Offaly was once an important cultural centre of early medieval Ireland.

LEFT: The Cross of the Scriptures and the 62-ft (19-m) round tower are just two of many relics of early medieval monastic life to be seen at Clonmacnoise, established on a remote stretch of the Shannon by St. Ciáran in the middle of the sixth century.

RIGHT: Scenes from the bible illustrate the tenth-century Celtic High Cross in the market square of the town of Clones, County Monaghan. Old Testament scenes are depicted on one side of the cross, while the reverse side illustrates stories from the New Testament.

OPPOSITE LEFT: The 75-ft (29-m) round tower stands in the grounds of the sixth-century monastery founded by St. Tighernach at Clones.

OPPOSITE RIGHT: The oldest building in Drumlane, Cavan, is the church and round tower on the banks of the River Erne. It is possibly late-13th century in date, although the first monastery here was founded in the early Christian period. It was much altered in the 15th century, its west doorway preserving some fine stonework.

churches are the remains of a large monastery founded in the sixth century by St. Diarmuid, and Saint's Island (now a peninsula), on which stand the ruins of a 14th-century Augustinian monastery. At lovely and peaceful Barley Harbour, tucked away at the end of a peninsula on the lough's eastern shore, is a haven popular with people cruising the lough and the Shannon; here the workshop of a sculptor, Michael Casey, can also be found, whose fine carvings in ancient, semi-petrified bog wood have earned him an international reputation.

HISTORICAL HIGHLIGHTS

Many names on the map of the Irish Midlands have strong historical associations. One with links to early Irish history, and with a place in Irish folklore as well, is the Rock of Dunamase, that rises out of the Laois countryside east of Port Laoise, the county town.

The rock is an ancient site, included on Ptolemy's famous map of AD 140, which has seen many battles for possession of the fortress on its summit. The Vikings plundered it, the Anglo-Normans built a castle on it, and the O'Moores, who had been clan chieftains in the area before the time of St. Patrick, built another, called Masg Castle (or Dun Masg), in the 15th century. This castle was destroyed by Cromwell's army in the 17th century, despite the presence, according to legend, of a huge mastiff called Bandog, whose flame-throwing jaws were said to be the animal's

means of protecting the treasure reputed to be buried beneath the rock. Perhaps Bandog's presence had some effect, for the castle was not completely destroyed, and its remains are still as attractive to visitors today.

A name closely associated with early Christian history in Ireland is that of Clonmacnoise in west Offaly. Here, one of the largest monasteries to be built in Ireland was founded by St. Ciáran, having sailed down the Shannon from his first monastery on Hare Island in Lough Ree in the mid sixth century. Carefully sited on a fertile meadow by the Shannon, its only access, apart from the river, being a ridgeway walk known as the Pilgrim's Road, the monastery survived and flourished as a centre of learning for 600 years.

Some of Ireland's finest illuminated manuscripts were produced at Clonmacnoise, including the 11th-century *Book of the Dun Cow* (*Lebor na hUidre*), the earliest-known manuscript to have been written in Irish, which took its name from a cow belonging to St. Ciáran. Another treasure from Clonmacnoise is the magnificent Crozier of Clonmacnoise, its golden handle inlaid with silver and decorated with the animals which once protected a saint's wooden staff. It can now be seen in the National Museum in Dublin.

The ruins at Clonmacnoise are extensive and well-preserved and include a cathedral, eight churches, a castle, two round towers and three high crosses. A collection of some 200 grave slabs, many inscribed with memorial prayers in Irish, can be seen in the Visitor Centre, together with the three high crosses, which have been replaced with replicas at their original locations.

One of the eight churches at Clonmacnoise was built by a chieftain's wife called Dervorgilla. It was her abduction by Dermot MacMurrough, King of Leinster, which led first to the king's overthrow, followed by his cry to the Anglo-Normans for help, who were only too ready to oblige him: Dervorgilla built her church in 1167, and the Anglo-Norman Strongbow was in Waterford with his army by 1169.

Two other Christian places in the region must also be mentioned. At one of them, Durrow Abbey, north of Tullamore in Offaly, little remains of a place referred to as a 'noble monastery' by the Venerable Bede. The abbey's greatest contribution to Irish culture, the *Book of Durrow*, a superbly illuminated manuscript dating from the seventh century, is now in the library of Trinity College, Dublin.

There is more to see at Fore, in the exceptionally lovely Fore Valley in County Westmeath. At Fore itself is an ancient church believed to date from the time when St. Fechin built a monastery here in around AD 630. Local legend has it that the saint himself placed the huge lintel, carved with a rare Greek cross, over the church's west door, having used the power of prayer to get it there. This feat is one of the 'Seven Wonders of Fore', which among others include such things as water that flows uphill, water that will

not boil, wood that will not burn, and a monastery built on quaking sod; the last is easily explained, for the Benedictine priory at Fore was built on reclaimed bogland. As for the rest, local people are happy to explain them, and the establishment of a regular tourist trail around them has also been discussed.

MUSIC IN IRELAND

There is a strong tradition of music-making in Ireland, guaranteed to lighten the heart and set the feet tapping. It is not the kind of music meant to be performed before an audience, which is expected to applaud politely once the piece is finished. Irish music means participation and this is what happens in pubs and bars, sessions (seisiúns) *and festivals* (fleadhs) *the length and breadth of the island.*

Traditional Irish music, grown out of the music-making and story-telling traditions of the bards of pre-Christian Celtic Ireland, has survived some fierce knocks over the centuries, not least the turbulent times of Cromwell and William III, when the bard's role in Irish music was all but extinguished, while the Potato Famine of the 19th century drove large parts of the rural-dwelling, music-making community abroad to the United States and the English-speaking colonies of the British Empire.

Today, traditional music thrives in Ireland, helped partly in the Republic by the government's sponsoring of Irish-language radio, and partly by a continuing dedication to ballad-singing in all those Irish communities abroad.

OPPOSITE: The religious foundations at Fore go back to St. Fechin in the seventh century. Fore Abbey, a Benedictine monastery located to the north of Lough Lene in County Westmeath, the lake-county of Ireland, was founded in the 13th century.

Musicians at a festival in Ennis, Clare, a county renowned for its music. Ennis hosts several festivals or fleadhs *every year.*

The establishment of Comhaltas Ceoltóirí Eireann (CCE) in the Republic in 1951, aimed at the promotion of traditional music, has also played a large part in helping the music to survive. There are now several hundred branches of the CCE, that organize regular informal sessions to which everyone is welcome. Larger than the sessions are the festivals, held all over Ireland, the greatest of which is the All-Ireland Fleadh, held at the end of August in a different town each year.

Details of sessions and festivals, as well as pub sessions, can be found in local newspapers and in tourist board listings. Keep an eye open as you walk past bars, too, as most of them put notices in their windows announcing forthcoming events. Depending on where you are in Ireland, the music on offer can be ballads, laments and airs; jigs, reels and hornpipes, taken from a national repertoire, according to a 1985 count, of which there are more than 6,000; and sean-nós, *a form of unaccompanied singing in Gaelic.*

The best traditional Irish music sessions to join are the smaller ones, where, if you are lucky and everyone is in the right mood, there will be a splendid mingling of music and 'crack' (good fun and conversation). Unless you are at an event organized by the tourist board, you are unlikely to hear the Irish harp being played, despite the fact that this ancient instrument is a national symbol. Instead, the music will be played on the uilleann *pipes (a more sophisticated version of Scotland's bagpipes), a fiddle, and a tin whistle, with a hand-held drum called a* bodhrán *providing the beat and rhythm. Some groups may also include guitar, accordian, flute and piano.*

Since the 1960s, this traditional Irish music scene has been taken to a much wider audience by musicians inspired by the traditional music band, The Cheftains, whose founder, Seán O'Riada, comes from Cuil Aodha, an Irish-speaking part of Ireland

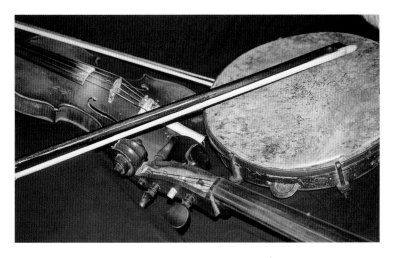

It is an echo that some Irish rock musicians may perhaps deny, maintaining that they are rebelling against traditional Irish music, that has been 'rammed down their throats from childhood'.

In fact, Irish music today, in whatever form, traditional, rock, pop or soul (the music celebrated in Alan Parker's splendid film (The Commitments), though firmly based in the past, is as enjoyable as ever and is a great part of the pleasure of making a visit to Ireland.

LEFT: The fiddle and bodhrán, its frame usually covered with goatskin, are important instruments used in traditional Irish music.

BELOW: Musicians perform traditional music most evenings on the Dingle Peninsula, Kerry, most notably at An Droichead Beag, where singing and set dancing are particularly encouraged.

famous for its singers. After them came the Clancy Brothers, in Aran sweaters, who took America by storm, and The Dubliners.

The tradition of music-making is so strong in Ireland that it is not surprising that the country has made a big contribution to other types of music as well. There were so many Irish winners of the Eurovision Song Contest in the 1980s that it began to look as though Dublin would soon be a permanent home of the event.

At the same time, Irish rock music was making its mark on the world's music scene, with singers like Van Morrison and Sinéad O'Connor and groups such as U2, the iconoclastic, punk London-Irish The Progues, and The Cranberries becoming hugely popular. The latter group's lead singer, Dolores O'Riordan, retains, like Van Morrison and Sinéad O'Connor at their best, strong echoes of the traditional Irish sean-nós in her singing.

CHAPTER FIVE
THE SOUTH-WEST
Cork & Kerry

FAR RIGHT: Seen from the air, Lough Leane is the largest of Killarney's lakes, with Macgillycuddy's Reeks beyond.

BELOW RIGHT: Rain can't dampen the spirits or the atmosphere at Cork's annual Guinness Jazz festival, held at the end of October each year.

OPPOSITE: A valley farm in the Shehy-Knockaboy area south-east of Kenmare in County Cork.

The coastlines of Cork and Kerry, at Ireland's south-western corner, reach out into the Atlantic in a series of jagged-edged peninsulas, all with islands at their tips, separated by long, wind- and sea-swept bays, inlets and river estuaries. Ranges of hills and mountains form barriers down the peninsulas, including the Caha Mountains on the Beara Peninsula, shared by Cork and Kerry; Macgillycuddy's Reeks, with Ireland's highest peaks, on the Iveragh Peninsula; and the Slieve Mish Mountains, which dominate the eastern end of the Dingle Peninsula. Further inland, the Boggeragh Mountains, with their scatterings of ring forts, standing stone circles and other prehistoric remains, separate the southern part of Cork, Ireland's largest county, from its north-western corner, being a remote, thinly populated area watered by the upper reaches of the Blackwater river.

RIGHT: Muckross House and its gardens, set in the splendidly car-free Muckross estate, is one of the highlights of a visit to Kerry's Killarney National Park.

OPPOSITE: The famous rose garden in Tralee's town park. Thanks to Kerry's mild climate there is also an abundance of subtropical plants, including bananas.

Despite the region's relatively easy access, by sea at least, to and from Europe – a fact recognized by invading Vikings and Anglo-Normans a thousand years and more ago, by Christian missionaries before that, and by such supporters of Irish rebellion as the Spanish and the French much later on – this part of Ireland was for many centuries a remote area, far removed from the influences of sophisticated society and intrusive government.

One result of this was the survival of the Irish language in the far west, long after it had either been suppressed or simply fallen out of use in favour of English elsewhere in the country. Today it is known as *Gaeltacht* or an Irish-speaking region, the language having survived particularly strongly in the Dingle and Iveragh Peninsulas in Kerry and near Macroom in County Cork. Irish culture, especially music and literature, thrives in the region today, and Irish language summer schools even attract students from Europe.

Tralee's famous Rose of Tralee International Festival and the annual Puck Fair at Killorglin, on the Ring of Kerry, show two, quite different present-day aspects of the south-west's Gaelic inheritance. Yet another aspect of this is the traditional music scene, that is alive and well in hundreds of pubs and clubs. Cork, especially, is renowned for its music, with traditional music very much to the fore in pubs and bars; this takes something of a back seat at the end of October every year, when the famous Cork International Jazz Festival gets into its stride.

LEAVING REMOTENESS BEHIND

The one part of the south-west which, in terms of location, could be seen as the most remote part of Ireland but which is in fact a magnet for visitors because of its extreme beauty, is Killarney. At the heart of County Kerry, this glorious land of island-studded lakes, wooded valleys, rolling hills and lush forest, 25,000 acres (10,000 hectares) of it in the Killarney National Park, has been the greatest tourist attraction in Ireland since the mid-18th century. First promoted as such by a local magnate, Lord Kenmare, in 1750, when the Romantic movement was beginning to take hold in Europe, Killarney proved to be the right place at the right time.

Although Killarney still holds the number one spot on Ireland's tourism chart, other parts of the south-west, notably the spectacular coastline, have been greatly increasing in popularity in recent years, both with the Irish themselves and with other Europeans. Visitors are more than eager to sample a country which combines beauty with an unhurried way of life, and where the influence of the Gulf Stream allows fragile wild flowers and the Mediterranean strawberry tree (arbutus) to flourish.

The south-west's long coastline, stretching from Youghal, an ancient fortified harbour and now a popular seaside resort on the Blackwater estuary, to Tarbert on the Limerick border, where the Shannon river reaches the sea, is heavily indented, creating hundreds of extra miles of bays, inlets, estuaries and harbours. While this coast has a rich maritime history and a strong tradition of fishing, still to be seen operating out of harbours from Dingle in County Kerry to Ballycotton in Cork, it is also a paradise for bird-watchers, for yachtsmen and for the many who like to walk on remote, unpopulated sandy beaches, where the only sounds are of the sea and of seabirds stalking the foreshore or wheeling in the sky above.

Maritime history and the pleasures of yachting come together in many small ports all along Cork's coast, notably at places like Youghal, Cobh and Kinsale. Cobh, Cork city's port, was once an important stopping-off place on the transatlantic shipping run and was for thousands of Irish emigrants to North America and Australia their last sight of their homeland. The *Sirius*, making the first steamer crossing of the Atlantic, began her epic trip from Cobh, and the ill-fated *Titanic* called here in 1912. In contrast, Cobh can also boast of once possessing the world's oldest yacht club, the Royal Cork, founded in 1720.

Kinsale is a characterful town with a colourful history, which includes the Battle of Kinsale in 1601, in which O'Donnell and O'Neill chieftains, aided by a Spanish force, made a last stand against English rule, only to be defeated. Kinsale is another sailing haven on the south coast to have experienced a tourist boom in recent years and its annual regatta is an important event in the social calendar of southern Ireland. Further west along the coast, places like Baltimore, sheltered behind Sherkin Island and with a boat-building yard and sailing school, and Skibbereen are

OPPOSITE: The town of Dingle lies below the Connor Pass in County Kerry.

PAGE 144: James's Fort, named after James I of England and VI of Scotland, is located on the Castlepark peninsula in Kinsale harbour in Cork, on the opposite side of the River Bandon from Kinsale and overlooking the town. Construction of the fort was begun in 1602, on the site of an earlier fortification, immediately after the Battle of Kinsale.

PAGE 145: Two views of the lighthouse on the Fastnet Rock, that rises from the Atlantic Ocean beyond Cape Clear in south-west Cork.

The world's oldest yacht club, the Royal Cork, may have moved across Cork Harbour to Crosshaven, but Cobh (pronounced 'Cove') remains a delightful yachting town.

harbours which attract yachts and small pleasure craft, while out to sea, beyond Sherkin Island and Clear Island, is a point of special interest to serious yachtsmen, the Fastnet Rock. This is the western turning point for one of the world's great yacht races, the Fastnet Race, which is held every two years and starts from Cowes on the Isle of Wight.

AROUND AND ABOUT CORK

Cork is Ireland's second largest city, a busy harbour, and the cultural capital of the south. Most of the city's business and shopping centre is built on an island, well inland of the River Lee's estuary, with many of the streets spanning former boat channels. The first famous settler here was St. Finbarr, who founded a monastery on the Lee in the seventh century. On the site of his monastery today is Cork's fine 19th-century Church of Ireland cathedral, its three Gothic spires rising above surrounding buildings near the Lee's southern channel.

Although Cork, unlike Dublin, has few places of importance to visitors, it is a most attractive city to explore. There are plenty of fine Georgian buildings, attractive quays and bridges to stroll along, with busy markets, one or two interesting art galleries, and plenty of pubs and bars. The Triskel Arts Centre is one of the main venues for Cork's important international film festival, held in early October each year. It is followed at the end of the month by the renowned Jazz Festival, making Cork a lively place.

Beyond Cork city's limits, County Cork stretches away in a semicircle of gentle landscape and fertile farmland, with rivers winding down heavily wooded valleys that offer much fine angling. Dotted across the landscape are some ancient castles, including the 15th-century Blarney Castle, where the famous Blarney Stone, set in the castle's battlements nearly 90ft (30m) above the ground, offers the gift of eloquence to anyone able to kiss it.

TO THE MEMORY OF ALL WHO PERISHED BY THE SINKING OF THE LUSITANIA MAY·7·1915 AND IN THE CAUSE OF UNIVERSAL AND LASTING PEACE

Memorial in Casement Square in the transatlantic port of Cobh in Cork Harbour, commemorating the sinking of Cunard's Lusitania *and the people who lost their lives, which was sunk by a German U-boat in 1915. Cobh (then Queenstown) was also the last port of call of the RMS* Titanic *on 4 April 1912 before she continued on her maiden voyage to New York. She never reached her destination, having struck an iceberg that caused her to sink on 14 April with a huge loss of life. There is a Titanic Trail in the town for those interested in the British Olympic-class ocean liner, which was the largest such vessel built at that time.*

OPPOSITE: St. Patrick's Street, in the heart of Cork city, has twice won an award as Ireland's best shopping street since its redevelopment in 2004.

LEFT: Parliament Bridge, looking over the south channel of the River Lee to old warehouses on George's Quay. It was built in 1806 to commemorate the Act of Union between Ireland and Great Britain.

BELOW: Looking across the River Lee's south channel from the bottom of Grand Parade south-west to Sullivan's Quay and St. Finbarr's Cathedral.

There are also some fine examples of the Anglo-Irish legacy in this part of the country. Near Cobh is the Fota Wildlike Park and Arboretum, in which many kinds of exotic animals, including apes, cheetah, giraffe and zebra, have the run of the 18th-century landscaped park which surrounds the classically elegant Fota House.

North of Cork and beyond the valley of the Blackwater river, in a quiet area known as the Golden Vale, where there are several

more castles and houses of interest, including the fine Doneraile Court, once home of the St. Leger family and another mansion whose fine parkland is home to a wildlife reserve, and Kilcolman Castle, once inhabited by Edmund Spenser and his family but a ruin since it was burned down by a mob in 1598: Spenser and his wife escaped the fire, but their infant son did not.

The horse is still king in this part of County Cork, with Buttevant, a market town 4 miles (6km) west of Doneraile, hosting the large Cahirmee Horse Fair each July. Both Buttevant and Doneraile hold important places in the history of Irish horse racing, for the first recognized steeplechase took place here in 1752, starting at Buttevant Church and finishing at St. Leger Church in Doneraile, the latter church's steeple providing a marker for the riders. Mallow, on the Blackwater, has one of the four important racecourses in the south-west, the other three being at Listowel, Tralee and Killarney.

Much further west, where Cork assumes the increasingly wild and far more elemental landscape typical of Ireland's south-west, Bantry House, overlooking the superb natural harbour of Bantry Bay, is another fine example of Irish Georgian architecture, still inhabited by the descendants of the earls of Bantry by whom it was built. From Bantry House's superb gardens, visitors can look across Bantry Bay to the Beara Peninsula where, beyond the Caha Mountains, County Kerry lies.

OPPOSITE RIGHT: St. Finbarr's, Cork's impressive Church of Ireland cathedral, was built in the mid-19th century to a design in the French Gothic style by William Burges. It is the third cathedral to be built on the site, though there have been chapels and churches here since the sixth century.

LEFT: Blarney Castle, County Cork. The Blarney Stone sits in the battlements at the top of the castle keep.

PAGE 152: Golfing on a summer evening on the southern shore of Bantry Bay, south-west of Bantry town, with the Caha Mountains in the distance.

PAGE 153: Situated on the seafront of the resort town of Ballybunnion, Kerry, are the remains of the castle of the Anglo-Norman Fitzmaurices, that was destroyed by fire in 1538. Listowel Castle to the south was also built by the Fitzmaurices.

THE KENMARE RIVER AND THE RING OF KERRY

The Kenmare river is an inlet of the sea, cutting a deep cleft into the coast of Kerry between the Beara and Iveragh Peninsulas. Other, smaller rivers and streams drain into it, notably the Finnihy, the Roughty and the Sheen near its head, and the Sneem which reaches the Kenmare near the pretty village of Sneem. On either side of the Kenmare rise mountains among which, on the southern side, lies the beautiful and tranquil Inchiquin Lough amid splendid scenery. There is a flourishing plantlife here, including, on the lough's southern shore, an area of primeval sessile oaks, known as Uragh Wood, and there is even a spectacular waterfall, falling from another lake in the hills above Inchiquin Lough. Because of the Gulf Stream, subtropical plants grow everywhere, with palm trees, yuccas, bamboos and fuchsias in profusion, alongside rhododendrons, the strawberry tree (arbutus), yellow gorse and green oaks and willows.

It is all so very charming that it is not surprising that villages like Sneem seem to have sprouted as many tourist cafés and gift shops as brightly-painted houses, while the resorts of Parknasilla, on the southern section of the Ring of Kerry, and Kenmare, a busy and attractive market town, seem far more cosmopolitan than one would have suspected. Although Kenmare is a fine example of 17th-century town planning, having been founded in 1670 by Cromwell's Surveyor-General in Ireland, Sir William Petty, it is in a place where many antiquities, including a 3,000-

Continued on page 169

THE SOUTH-WEST

RIGHT: Looking south over Castleisland and the valley of the River Maine in the north of Kerry. The town, once the centre of Desmond power, got its name, Castle of the Island of Kerry, from a castle built in 1226 by the then Lord Justice of Ireland during the reign of Henry III. The island was created by turning the waters of the River Maine into a moat surrounding the castle.

OPPOSITE: Carrigafoyle Castle, a large tower house of a type common in north Munster, was built by Conor Liath O'Connor-Kerry in the 1490s, and was considered to be one of the strongest fortresses in Ireland. It stands inside its bawn on the Shannon estuary near Ballylongford in Kerry. The siege of Carrigafoyle Castle took place in 1580, the engagement being part of the English crown's campaign against the forces of the 15th Earl of Desmond during the Second Desmond Rebellion.

155

RIGHT: A mountainside cottage near Moll's Gap between Killarney and Kenmare.

OPPOSITE: Twin corner towers are all that remain of the once imposing Listowel Castle in Kerry, the last bastion against Queen Elizabeth I, falling to an English force after a 28-day siege in 1600. Listowel Castle was built by the Anglo-Norman Fitzmaurices, the Knights of Kerry, in the 12th century and was of tremendous strategic importance to them since they were constantly feuding not only with the Desmonds and the O'Neills, but also with the crown forces. It became the property of the earls of Listowel after reverting from the Fitzmaurices. It is now a national monument.

157

OPPOSITE: A rain squall over Inch Strand, the Dingle Peninsula, Kerry, looking towards Iveragh. The beach stretches 5 miles (8km) into Dingle Bay and was the location for the films Ryan's Daughter *and* The Playboy of the Western World.

LEFT: In recent years, Ireland's housing boom has caused the traditional Irish cottage to be replaced by new developments, such as the one at Abbydorney, in north Kerry.

OPPOSITE: A view of Galway's river from Galway's Bridge, that flows into Upper Lake in Killarney National Park, Kerry.

LEFT: A boatman on Upper Lake, Killarney National Park.

RIGHT: The beach at Brandon Bay, one of the top windsurfing locations in Ireland, stretches for several miles from Fahamore to Kilcummin on the north side of the Dingle Peninsula.

OPPOSITE: The rugged edge of the Iveragh Peninsula at Dromgour dips into the Atlantic south of Bray Head, Valencia.

RIGHT: The beehive-shaped huts are remains of an early monastic settlement on Skellig Michael.

FAR RIGHT: A sculpture 'To the Skellig', by Eamon Doherty, depicting four monks in a boat going to the monastic island of Skellig Michael.

OPPOSITE: The island of Skellig Michael, off the west coast of Kerry, is one of the most enigmatic and remote sacred sites in all of Europe, having been an important centre of monastic life for 600 years. The Irish Celtic monastery, situated almost at the summit of the rock, was built in 588, and became a UNESCO World Heritage Site in 1996.

RIGHT: View from Skellig Michael's carved-out steps of the island of Little Skellig, now an important seabird colony.

OPPOSITE: Dunquin's small, sheltered harbour services boats going to and from the Blasket Islands at the western tip of the Dingle Peninsula.

RIGHT: Double the luck! A shamrock made from horseshoes on a door at Slea Head, Kerry.

FAR RIGHT: A standing stone on the summit of Dunmore Head above Blasket Sound bears inscriptions in ogham, an ancient Irish and British alphabet, cut into its corners.

OPPOSITE: The low tide uncovers the fine sandy beach beneath Slea Head.

year-old stone circle, attest to long habitation. The lace-making industry for which Kenmare, guided by the nuns of the local convent of Poor Clares, became famous in Victorian times is undergoing something of a revival today.

One reason why Kenmare has so many visitors in summer is because it is on the Ring of Kerry, one of the world's great scenic routes. This circles the Iveragh Peninsula, with its spectacular mountain and coastal scenery and its crowning glory, the Killarney National Park. The Ring of Kerry is just about everything expected of a world-famous region of supreme natural beauty.

There are other fine resorts, like Waterville, once a favourite holiday haunt of Charlie Chaplin and his family, Valencia Island, reached by a modern bridge from Portmagee and able to claim that it is the most westerly harbour in Europe, and Derrynane, whose wide sandy beaches stretch for miles. There is the amazingly well-preserved Staigue Fort near Caherdaniel, one of the best in Ireland, while the island group, the Skelligs, are within a pleasure boat's cruising distance off the tip of the peninsula. Skellig Michael offers the hardy tourist, via a 500-ft (150-m) climb up a stone stairway, built a thousand years ago, a view of a particularly magnificent monastic site, complete with some remarkably well-preserved stone beehive huts in which the monks once lived. Little Skellig is a seabird sanctuary, home to hundreds of thousands of gannets, kittiwakes, petrels and their like.

OPPOSITE: The early Christian round tower at Rattoo, south of Ballybunnion, rises to 92ft (28m) beside the ruins of a church.

LEFT: The Torc Waterfall in the wooded glen of the Owengarrif river beside Muckross Lake and Abbey, Killarney. It is only one of many waterfalls in the area but it is certainly the most famous.

THIS PAGE & OPPOSITE:
Brightly painted shops and houses
are de rigueur not only in
Castlegregory, a village on the
north side of the Dingle Peninsula,
halfway between Tralee and Dingle,
but also in Dingle itself.

THE DINGLE PENINSULA

While the Dingle Peninsula cannot offer the same dramatic impact as the Iveragh Peninsula, it has for many an attraction all its own, not least the wonderful peace of its splendid landscape, which includes the Connor Pass, Ireland's highest mountain pass. This seems especially so at the height of summer, when the jaunting cars block the roads out of Killarney, and the way to every lake, every tourist site, every view becomes a slow-moving

OPPOSITE: Seen from Connor Hill, the old mountain road rises from the town of Dingle, with the mountains of Iveragh behind.

LEFT: The ruined walls of an old farmstead subside back into the landscape in the valley head south of Brandon Peak, Dingle Peninsula.

RIGHT & FAR RIGHT: The Gallarus Oratory has survived the elements in this remote part of the Dingle Peninsula for over 1,000 years. Built as a place for quiet, private prayer, the Oratory remains a moving and evocative Christian site. The picture on the right of the page shows the Oratory's fine corbelled drystone construction.

trek: it is much more agreeable to think about hiring a horse-drawn caravan in Tralee and take off at a gentle pace to discover the Dingle Peninsula.

It is easy to feel you have gone back in time. This is partly due to the remoteness and peace of the place and partly because the peninsula west of Dingle town is *Gaeltacht*, where Gaelic is the first language of most of the inhabitants. There are also something like 2,000 prehistoric and early Christian sites to be found here, evoking an overriding sense of history and of the past. Among the finest of these is the extraordinarily atmospheric Gallarus Oratory, a remarkable little drystone building shaped like an upturned boat, its interior lit by one small window and a narrow door. Set in a field a short distance inland from Smerwick harbour, the oratory is thought to have been built between 800 and 1200.

The solitariness of the Gallarus Oratory seems a world away from the busy, colourful life of Dingle, the fishing port and tourist centre on the south side of the peninsula. Dingle, which for walkers wishing to take their time getting there, is 20 miles (32km) from Tralee via the Dingle Way; it has had an eventful history, including a period when it was a centre for smuggling. Among its tourist attractions today is a dolphin called Fungie who has been delighting spectators with his antics since 1984.

Tralee, at the head of Tralee Bay on the northern edge of the Dingle Peninsula, is County Kerry's chief town. It lies in the lovely fertile Vale of Tralee, celebrated in the song 'The Rose of Tralee', which gives its name to the Rose of Tralee International Festival. Fenit, west of Tralee on the north shore of Tralee Bay, was the birthplace of St. Brendan the Navigator, and legend has it that Brendan began his epic voyage in a curach (curragh) to cross the Atlantic to North America from the south coast of the Dingle Peninsula. In 1976–77, the British writer/adventurer Tim Severin

The fishing port of Dingle in west Kerry is famous for its pubs, music and relaxed atmosphere.

proved that the saint could have done this by building a replica boat of wood and leather 36ft (11m) long, which he named the *Brendan*, and sailing it across the Atlantic, retracing Brendan's original route.

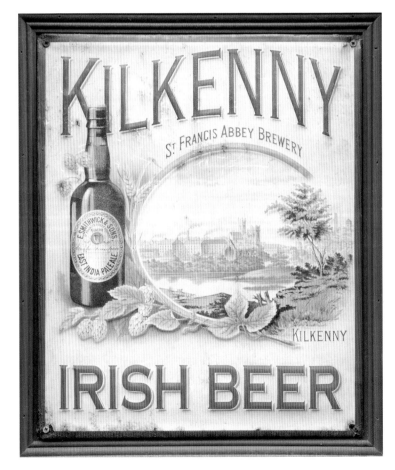

OPPOSITE LEFT: The Blasket Islands can be seen outlined on the horizon from Clougher Strand on the Dingle Peninsula.

OPPOSITE RIGHT: An old enamel sign seen outside a bar in Tralee.

LEFT: A swan with cygnets on Lough Gill near Castlegregory on the Dingle Peninsula.

RIGHT: Much of the country in the rugged Comeragh Mountains, in the north of County Waterford, is of the same red sandstone that lies under the scenic parts of Cork and Kerry.

OPPOSITE: The ruined walls of an old farmstead are all that remain of civilization in the valleys near Brandon Peak in Kerry.

WILD IRELAND

Ireland packs into its relatively small size an extraordinary variety of scenery and many areas of unspoiled grandeur. There are some 2,000 miles of coast, with hundreds of islands scattered offshore, including some very wild coast indeed in the south-west, where the land reaches out into the Atlantic Ocean in a series of finger-like peninsulas, whose cliffs and rock stacks provide havens for many colonies of birds.

Away from the coast is a country of glorious contrasts: mountains in the west, with much of the land between covered by blanket bog, one of the finest examples of which lies in the Slieve Bloom Mountains in Laois and Offaly; green and purple hills and valleys; and, at the island's centre, a fertile lowland region of wetlands and lakes watered by many lovely rivers and streams. Very little is left of the great broadleaf forests which once covered much of the land, and the long-distance views are likely to be filled with lush, rolling pasture, the result of plentiful rainfall, divided into a checkerboard of hedge-lined fields where livestock graze.

Much of Ireland's farming, especially in the west, is still practised along traditional lines, which is of great value in helping wildlife to survive in good numbers. Ireland was cut off from the rest of the British Isles and Europe by rising sea levels after the last Ice Age, and many animals, common in Europe, are unknown in Ireland as a result.

You won't encounter any snakes when walking in Irish grassland, for instance, neither will you see moles, weasels, the common toad or any small rodents other than the wood mouse. Red squirrels are

BELOW: Ireland's coastline, with its long stretches of rugged cliffs broken by river estuaries and sand dunes, provides homes for many kinds of seabirds, including puffins, which nest in large colonies on rocky cliff sites.

more in evidence than the grey, for the former are more widespread, while in hill country, especially in Connemara, there is an introduced species of red deer.

On remote beaches on western islands grey seals breed and sometimes that nocturnal animal, the otter, may be seen during the day, so undisturbed are these places. Although the otter's preferred

habitat is the shallow sea off rocky coasts, it has also been seen on Ireland's inland waterways.

For many nature-lovers, however, the great interest of Ireland lies in its birdlife, and this is abundant both on the coasts and along inland waterways. From the cliffs of the extreme west, where the chough still breeds well while declining in the rest of Europe, to the mudflats and salt marshes of east- and south-coast river estuaries, which attract spectacular flocks of wading birds and wildfowl, including Brent geese, curlews, redshanks and teal, Ireland is a bird-watcher's paradise.

When observing colonies of breeding seabirds, including kittiwakes, shags, Manx shearwaters, gannets and several different types of gull, you should be positioning yourself on some west-facing headland in early summer, where you might even be rewarded with dolphins or porpoises coming within sight of land.

Ireland's rivers and central wetlands, created by the high annual rainfall, offer breeding grounds for many kinds of water birds, including swans, herons and moorhens. Along the Shannon and the Erne rivers are many areas of bird-attracting wetland, and the larger lakes in the north offer breeding grounds for birds such as the elegant great crested grebe.

There are five national parks in the Republic of Ireland, and because they are mainly state-owned, unlike Britain's, they are not very big. What they lack in size, however, they more than make up for in the varied nature of their landscapes and geology and the richness of their fauna and flora. The five parks are the Glenveagh National Park, set in the spectacular mountain ranges of County Donegal; the small but carefully conserved Connemara National Park in County Galway; the beautiful, lake-dominated Killarney National Park in Kerry; the Wicklow National Park; and the strangely austere and even bleak Burren National Park in County Clare, where the limestone grassland gives shelter to an extraordinary collection of wildflowers, from arctic-alpine species to Mediterranean ferns. The Burren Way, that can be completed by walkers in two days, offers a dramatic path through The Burren and

along the tops of one of Ireland's most spectacular sights, the Cliffs of Moher.

Northern Ireland, while it has no national parks, does have several officially designated areas of outstanding natural beauty, offering a superb introduction to its scenic beauties by way of the Ulster Walk, a complete circuit of the six counties nearly 560 miles (900km) long. And Northern Ireland's scenic beauties are well worth discovering, from the lovely Mourne Mountains, where there are moves to establish the Province's first national park, to the spectacular piles of basalt that make up the Giant's Causeway on the northern coast of County Antrim.

OPPOSITE RIGHT: A gannet guards its young on one of the Saltee Islands, off Kilmore Quay in Co. Wexford. The Saltees are some of Ireland's most significant bird sanctuaries, supporting colonies of gannets, cormorants, kittiwakes, auks and puffins.

BELOW: One of many stretches of unspoilt beach and coastline on the Dingle Peninsula.

OPPOSITE: Sheep graze the cliffs high above the Atlantic at Slieve League in Donegal.

LEFT: An aerial view of the Island of Inishtravin in Kilkieran Bay, Connemara, Galway. This harsh rugged landscape, in spite of taking a battering from the Atlantic, is still used as grazing land.

CHAPTER SIX
THE WEST
Limerick, Clare, Galway, Mayo, Roscommon

FAR RIGHT: A Station of the Cross in the Trinitarian Abbey, Adare, Limerick, founded by the Fitzgeralds in 1230.

BELOW: Carved stone heads on the door of the ancient monastic church at Dysert O'Dea, Co. Clare.

OPPOSITE: Connemara ponies below the range of the Twelve Bens in Galway.

*I*reland's western counties, though they have much in common, not least in their long stretches of dramatic coastline and, as far as history goes, a certain remoteness from the affairs of government in the east, also have their own distinctly different atmospheres. The counties in the south, Limerick and Clare, share the lower reaches of the River Shannon and its largest lake, Lough Dergh, as their outstanding geographical features, while the area bordering the Shannon, Ireland's longest river, much of which has great beauty, has known human habitation for at least 7,000 years: a canoe, recently found in the Shannon estuary mudflats, has been

St. Veronica wipes our Lord's face.

OPPOSITE: Bunratty Castle, in County Clare, is a large tower house lying in the centre of Bunratty village between Limerick and Ennis, near Shannon town and its airport.

LEFT: Horse dealers, returning from Ballinasloe Fair, rest on the bridge below Ballylee Castle, once the home, near Gort, Galway, of the poet W.B. Yeats,

PAGE 190: The classroom at Bunratty Folk Park, adjacent to Bunratty Castle. The aim of the park is to show what everyday life was like in rural Ireland about 100 years ago. It contains reconstructed farmhouses, cottages and shops, and care has been taken to make them as authentic as possible.

PAGE 191 LEFT: Curiosities on display at Bunratty Castle.

PAGE 191 RIGHT: Detail of a wood carving in Bunratty Castle's great hall.

BELOW: Pages from traditional poetry books in the window of Foster's Printworks in Bunratty.

FAR RIGHT: Bunratty Castle: the solar room, with its elaborate Tudor-style ceiling and original furniture.

carbon-dated to 4800 BC, which sets it in the mesolithic period. From about the fifth century AD, this area was part of the province of Munster, though the seat of the kings of Munster was further away, on the Rock of Cashel in present-day Tipperary. More recently, it has become increasingly popular with visitors and holidaymakers attracted to its numerous riverside resorts.

A demonstration of traditional corn-threshing performed by veterans in Bunratty's Folk Park.

OPPOSITE: The Desmond Castle (Adare Castle), on the River Maigue in Limerick, predates the arrival of the Normans in the 12th century and is said to have been built by the O'Donovans. It was the property of the Fitzgeralds, the earls of Kildare, for nearly 300 years until 1536, when it was forfeited and granted to the earls of Desmond, who gave the castle its present name.

FAR LEFT: Young girls dancing in traditional Irish folk-dancing costumes at the Bunratty Folk Park, County Clare.

LEFT: One of the 12th-century High Crosses in the vicinity of St. Fachnan's Cathedral in the village of Kilfenora, County Clare.

RIGHT: A traditional music session in Day's Bar on the island of Inishbofin, 7 miles (11km) off the coast of Galway.

OPPOSITE: The Poulnabrone Dolmen, a megalithic tomb, was erected on the karstic limestone pavement of The Burren, in County Clare, some 4,500 years ago.

THE WEST

Away from the Shannon, Limerick and Clare seem quiet counties, and provide a breathing space for tourists hurrying from the scenic glories of Kerry to those of Galway. But Limerick has in its county town of Limerick, founded by Norsemen, the only urban area of city size in the region – in fact, Limerick is the fourth largest city in Ireland. County Clare is famous for the liveliness of its music scene and both counties can offer many attractions along their spectacular jagged coastlines, not least Clare's Cliffs of Moher and The Burren, and the Aran Islands, scattered across the mouth of Galway Bay.

What most people imagine to be the typical west-of-Ireland landscape is in fact to be found further north, in Galway, Mayo and Roscommon, once the heart of the historic province of Connaught. Bordered by a rugged coastline is a sparsely

OPPOSITE LEFT: From Croagh Patrick, Co. Mayo, Ireland's holiest mountain and colloquially known as the Reek, there is a splendid view across the island-studded Clew Bay.

OPPOSITE RIGHT: An Irish-language sign above the post office door on the island of Inishbofin off the coast of Galway.

FAR LEFT: Young musicians play for dancers outside the village pub at Bunratty, Clare.

LEFT: The 15th-century Feartagar Castle, known locally as Jennings Castle, near Tuam, Galway. Once a stronghold of the Burke family, it has lain abandoned since the 1650s.

OPPOSITE: O'Brien's Tower sits on top of the Cliffs of Moher, and was built by a local landlord, Cornelius O'Brien, in 1835, so that visitors, who were already flocking to the cliffs, would have a more splendid view. On a clear day, it is possible to see as far as Loop Head, on the southernmost tip of County Clare, and beyond to the mountains of Kerry, while to the north can be seen the Aran Islands in Galway Bay and as far away as the Twelve Bens (Twelve Pins) and the Maumturk Mountains in Connemara.

LEFT: The Cliffs of Moher, composed of horizontal layers of sandstone and black shale, are one of Ireland's most outstanding coastal features and a haven for seabirds. They rise almost vertically to over 700ft (213m) only 3 miles (5km) south of the village of Doolin, in County Clare.

RIGHT: Fine country hotels and golf courses seem to go hand-in-hand in Ireland. The 19th-century Adare Manor is located on the banks of the River Maigue in the village of Adare, County Limerick. Sold in 1987, it was restored by an Irish-American businessman and converted into the Adare Manor Hotel. The Adare Golf Club was added alongside in 1995 and has been hosting the Irish Open since 2007.

OPPOSITE: Leameneh Castle, in County Clare, was once the seat of the powerful O'Brien clan. A 17th-century mansion was built into the side of the massive tower which dates from 1480.

populated land of dour bracken-covered hills, peat bogs, and fields divided by stone walls, which typifies the landscape of Connemara in the west of Galway. Inland, where Galway and Mayo merge into Roscommon, lies extensive and fertile agricultural and cattle-rearing country, dotted with quiet lakes.

But these western counties are changing, too. These days, the medieval streets of Galway town resound to the voices of students at its thriving university college and of workers in the new high-tech industries which have been developed there. And at nearby Knock, a quiet little village in the middle of a bog in

County Mayo only 100 years ago, an airport, Ireland West Airport Knock, previously Connaught, was built in 1986 – now the fastest-growing airport in the country. Most of the visitors come to worship at the shrine of Knock, where in 1879 two local women are reputed to have seen visions of the Virgin Mary, St. Joseph and St. John the Evangelist; but there are also increasing numbers of people using the airport to visit Ireland's west country.

AROUND THE LOWER SHANNON

For other modern travellers, the first sight of Ireland may well be the broad sweep of the estuary of the Shannon, seen from the air as their aircraft, flying in from over the Atlantic, makes its approach to Shannon International, the world's first duty-free airport. In fact it is historic aviation country here, for Foynes, on the south coast of the estuary, was in the 1930s the European airbase for the transatlantic flying-boat service to Newfoundland.

This area has a history much longer than that of modern aviation, of course. There are several important archeological sites in the region, notably round Lough Gur, south of Limerick, which is one of north-west Europe's most complete Stone Age and Bronze Age sites, where a gallery grave dating from 2000 BC, stone circles, forts, and the foundations of many huts are still to be seen. The barren limestone country of The Burren, further north in County Clare, also has many megalithic remains, of

which the best-known, the Poulnabrone Dolmen (page 197), has been dated to 2500 BC.

His engagement in excavations around Lough Gur inspired the archeologist John Hunt to create his own prehistoric site in County Clare, the intention being to provide the people of Ireland with an insight into how their Celtic ancestors lived in the Bronze Age. Today, the Craggaunowen Project, created in the grounds of Craggaunowen Castle at Kilmurry, is a very fine example of how past history can be vividly recreated for our

OPPOSITE: One of Adare's pretty 'English' thatched cottages.

FAR LEFT: A carved stone effigy in the cathedral at Kilfenora, Clare, possibly of St. Fachnan.

BELOW: Shrine of the Virgin Mary in the Trinitarian Abbey, now fully restored as Adare's Catholic Church, Limerick.

RIGHT: The modern development of the Howley and Bishop's Quays on the River Shannon below Sarsfield Bridge, Limerick.

OPPOSITE: King John's Castle. The Viking city of Limerick acquired further dominance over the Shannon area when King John founded his massive castle here in 1212.

RIGHT: Foynes, a small town and major port on the southern bank of the Shannon estuary in Limerick, was a major transatlantic seaplane base prior to the development of Shannon Airport.

OPPOSITE: Neolithic fields excavated from peat at the Céide Fields, Mayo, reveal man's earliest transition from hunter-gatherer to farmer.

PAGE 210: The village of Slievemore, on Achill Island, Mayo, was abandoned as a consequence of Ireland's Great Famine of the 1850s.

benefit. Visitors can see people in the costume of the period, engaged in activities such as spinning, potting and cooking, and they can walk around a typical crannog – a man-made island, built as a defensive dwelling, usually in a lake and enclosing wattle-and-daub houses which were still being built in Ireland up to the end of the 16th century. Also at Craggaunowen is Tim Severin's *Brendan*, in which he re-enacted the sixth-century voyage of St. Brendan the Navigator to North America.

Signs of early Christian settlement are also to be found here, including a sixth-century monastery founded by St. Senan on Scattery Island, off the southern coast of Clare near Kilrush, the county's second largest town and an important trading centre. Later religious orders, notably the Cistercians, founded numerous monasteries in the region, while in more modern times there are many historic buildings in the area, covering a wide range of architectural styles and periods.

Killaloe, County Clare, in a lovely setting where the Shannon flows out of Lough Dergh, is today a fine pleasure resort and boating centre, but it also has a lot of history behind it, not least in its impressive St. Flannan's Cathedral, which includes among its treasures an unusual stone, which is inscribed in ogham (the earliest Irish and British script) and with Nordic runes.

Cratloe House, west of Limerick, is a rare example of an Irish long house in which all the rooms are interconnecting. The

whole of the Bunratty Folk Park, on the road from Limerick to Shannon Airport, has many important buildings, including the formidable Bunratty Castle, recently magnificently restored and offering medieval banquets to tourists and a complete 19th-century village street. The pretty town of Adare, south of Limerick, has many interesting buildings, including a 14th-

FAR LEFT: Aasleagh Falls, where salmon leap on the Erriff river, east of Leenaun, Mayo.

BELOW: The turf-fired power station at Bellacorick, Mayo, surrounded by vast peat bogs.

RIGHT: Fine stone carvings from the 12th-century Cistercian abbey at Boyle, Roscommon.

OPPOSITE: The 12th-century St. Tola's Celtic Christian High Cross stands before a medieval monastic church at Dysert O'Dea, Clare.

RIGHT: The cloisters of the Franciscian friary at Quin in County Clare date from 1402. The friary was founded in 1402 by Sioda Cam Mac Namara, and incorporates the walls of a strong Anglo-Norman castle built by Thomas de Clare.

OPPOSITE: Aughnanure Castle, County Galway, was built by the O'Flahertys in the 16th century with a rounded turret at the corner of the surrounding inner bawn. It was used to blockade Galway during the Cromwellian invasion.

PAGE 216: Looking north to the range of Nephin Beg in Mayo, the evening rain-clouds arriving from the Atlantic to gather over the islands of Clew Bay.

PAGE 217: The popular town of Westport at the head of Clew Bay.

century Augustinian abbey (now Church of Ireland), a Trinitarian priory (used by Catholic worshippers) and numerous 19th-century thatched cottages.

Limerick itself was a Viking settlement, established in the ninth century on an island between the Shannon and the smaller Abbey river, which the Anglo-Normans turned into a thriving town. They embellished it with some splendid buildings, including the superb St. Mary's Cathedral and King John's Castle (page 207), both prominent buildings in the town today. The castle has had a turbulent history, having been subjected to capture by the unruly O'Briens, kings of Thomond, in the 13th century, bombardments by Cromwell's General Ireton, and attacks by William of Orange's troops later on in the 17th century.

County Clare's county town is Ennis, and though much smaller than Limerick it remains an attractive town with many brightly-painted houses and shops, its winding lanes recalling its medieval origins, of which the ruined but still impressive Ennis Friary is the main survivor today. Ennis was another town of the O'Briens, and their rebellious spirit lived on well after their passing, so that Ennis remained a proud bastion of Irish nationalism even in the 19th century. The town's main street and main square are named after Daniel O'Connell, The Liberator, who was elected Member of Parliament for Clare in 1828. A monument to him dominates O'Connell Square.

BELOW: Site of the Battle of Aughrim, fought between the Jacobites and the forces of William III on 12 July 1691 near the village of Aughrim in County Galway.

GALWAY BAY: THE ARAN ISLANDS

There are three Aran Islands, Inishmore, at 8 miles (13km) from end to end the largest, Inishmaan and Inisheer, *inish* being the Irish word for 'island'. The islands, stretched across the mouth of Galway Bay, are the peaks of a ridge extending from the limestone country of The Burren in County Clare.

OPPOSITE RIGHT: Teetering on the edge: the concentric rings of the prehistoric fort of Dún Aengus were built on the cliffs rising 300ft (90m) out over the Atlantic on Inishmore, largest of the three Aran Islands.

LEFT: The Dún Eoghanachta stone fort (cashel) in the limestone landscape of Inishmore, in Galway Bay.

PAGE 220: Crystal-clear waters and white sands at Tramore on Inishmore.

PAGE 221: The wreck of the freighter Plenney, *marooned high on the rocky shore of Inisheer, the smallest of the Aran Islands.*

The ancient church of St. Cavan (Kenelm or Kevin), now half buried in sand dunes on the Aran Island of Inisheer.

Despite, or perhaps because of their isolated position, the islands have long been inhabited. There are prehistoric stone forts scattered across all three islands; Dún Aengas (page 218 right), a great Bronze Age fort on Inishmore's southern coast, with three concentric stone walls and a ring of spiked stone stakes as its defences, is recognized today as one of the great prehistoric sites of Europe. Christian missionaries were also here in early times, St. Enda having arrived in the fifth century to begin a long tradition of austere monasticism. The saint, after a lifetime of teaching, is said to have been buried on the site of his monastery, where the ruins of the later St. Eany's Church are still to be found, south of Kilronan, the island's main town and port.

LEFT: Dún Dúchathair, the 'black castle', is an ancient stone promontory fort, set high on the southern limestone cliffs of Inishmore. It contains the remnants of several 'beehive' huts.

PAGE 224: A typical Connemara lanscape of rocky terrain, tidal inlets and small lakes.

Like the Blasket Islands, off the Dingle Peninsula, where the Gaelic literary tradition has influenced modern Irish writing, the Aran Islands, with their continuing observance of traditional Irish culture and use of the Gaelic language, has also had a notable influence on modern Irish literature, especially drama; J.M. Synge was inspired by stories of the Aran Islands to write *Riders to the Sea*, set on Inishmaan, and *The Playboy of the Western World*. A present-day writer to be influenced by the life of the islands is the playwright Martin McDonagh, whose recent

FAR LEFT: Des O'Halloran, an accomplished singer and fiddle player on Inishbofin, Galway.

BELOW: A Galway hooker, a traditional sailing, fishing and cargo boat, entering the harbour at Kinvara on Galway Bay.

RIGHT: *The shop and gallery in Recess, Connemara.*

OPPOSITE: *Children on their way home to Roundstone, Connemara. The village is set on one of the most spectacular coastal drives in Europe, situated at the foot of Errisbeg Mountain and overlooking the Atlantic Ocean.*

BELOW & RIGHT: A little paint and some imagination has been used to great effect in the fishing village of Kinvara on the southern shore of Galway Bay.

play, *The Cripple of Inishmaan*, is based on the arrival on Inishmore in 1934 of the great documentary film-maker, Robert Flaherty, come to film *Man of Aran*.

Today, as everywhere else, the Aran Islands are no longer remote, and all three islands have airstrips and ferry services from Rossaveel and Galway in County Galway and Doolin in Clare: but the old way of life, so superbly recorded by Flaherty, is fast

LEFT: A summer evening in the busy town of Clifden on the west coast of Galway.

PAGE 230: Looking north over the tidal inlets of Black Haven, north of Roundstone, to the backdrop of the Twelve Bens (Pins) mountains in Connemara.

PAGE 231: The picturesque fishing village of Roundstone on the west side of Bertraghboy Bay, Connemara.

disappearing into a world of heritage centres (there is one in Kilronan) and the business of keeping tourists occupied and happy. But while tourism, complete with jaunting cars, minibus tours and bikes for hire, is today an important money-earner for the Aran Islands, older occupations, including fishing, farming and the production of the distinctive Aran knitwear, continue to flourish.

AROUND GALWAY

The city of Galway is the gateway to Ireland's most extensive region of *Gaeltacht*, and includes the Aran Islands, Connemara and Joyce Country. It is a lively university city with a flourishing arts scene and a busy port. It is also undergoing something of a modern high-tech industrial revolution, all of which makes Galway's county town and the biggest conurbation in the west of Ireland a place well worth visiting. It has an attractive city centre, built along the banks of the River Corrib, its own 'Latin Quarter', and a quieter area called The Quays, where Spanish traders once unloaded their ships' cargoes. There is a fine medieval church, the Collegiate Church of St. Nicholas, where Columbus heard Mass before setting out across the Atlantic in search of the New World, as St. Brendan the Navigator had done before him.

Galway, along with Clifden on the Connemara coast and Westport in County Mayo, are popular with visitors and tourists as bases from which to explore the glories of the region.

OPPOSITE: Eyre Square, in Galway city, with a sculpture of a Galway hooker sailboat and the doorway of the Browne Merchant House dating from 1627.

LEFT: A wayside shrine to the Virgin Mary near Recess, Connemara.

BELOW: Outside Tigh Neachtain (Naughton's Pub), on Cross Street, in Galway's lively and atmospheric Spanish Arch (Latin Quarter) district.

In the attractive countryside to the east and south of Galway, there are many historically interesting places to visit, ranging from the delightful fishing village of Kinvara, on Galway Bay, to the inland market town of Portumna. South of Galway is Gort, famous for its associations with W.B. Yeats. His friend, Lady Gregory, with whom he founded the Abbey Theatre in Dublin,

OPPOSITE RIGHT: Goatskin-covered bodhrans *or Irish drums. They are made by master craftsman Malachy Kearns, who sells them from his workshop in Roundstone.*

LEFT: The night life around the pubs and restaurants on Quay Street, Galway.

OPPOSITE LEFT: Quay Street, in Galway city, is full of shops, pubs and restaurants.

OPPOSITE RIGHT: Plenty of crack and live music downstairs at The Quays pub on Quay Street.

LEFT: Looking across Loch Bhaile na hinse to the Twelve Bens, west of Recess, Connemara.

PAGE 238: The fine sandy beach at Gorteen Bay, near Roundstone, on Connemara's south-western coast.

lived at nearby Coole Park, while also on the Gregory estate is Thoor Ballylee, a tower house which belonged to Yeats and where he and his family spent their summers for many years.

Anglers and seekers of peace and tranquillity tend to head north out of Galway to island-dotted Lough Corrib, one of the chain of loughs which divides the wilder, western side of Galway and Mayo from the fertile eastern farmlands. Walkers and ramblers, along with watersports enthusiasts, tend to head for the islands, including, away to the north off Mayo's coast, Achill Island, which is Ireland's largest island and connected to the mainland by a road bridge, and Clare Island in Clew Bay, once the stronghold of a pirate queen called Grace O'Malley. But for most visitors, the region not to be missed is Connemara.

Bogland, lakes and mountains, dominated by the peaks of the Twelve Bens, watered by tumbling streams and fringed by a wild and rugged coastline, are all unforgettable features of the Connemara landscape. Some of the most spectacular scenery, including four of the Twelve Bens, lies within the boundary of the 5,000-acre (2,000-hectare) Connemara National Park. Here, Connemara ponies roam, along with red deer, re-introduced into the area, and there is a wide variety of birds. There are signposted walks and botanists are available to describe the flora to visitors, which includes Mediterranean, alpine and subarctic species.

Part of the National Park was once within the estate of Kylemore Abbey, a wildly romantic Gothic castle built by a

wealthy Manchester businessman in the 19th century on the shores of Kylemore Lough, on the north-eastern edge of the National Park. The fantasy castle became an abbey during the First World War, when a group of Benedictine nuns from Belgium took refuge there. The nuns are still there today, where they run a convent school.

Kylemore Abbey, on the shores of Kylemore Lough in Co. Galway, was built in the Gothic style in the 19th century. It is now a girls' school.

OPPOSITE: Stormy Atlantic weather. The lighthouse marks the treacherous rocks of Slyne Head at the south-western tip of Connemara.

LEFT: East of Leenaun at the head of Killary harbour in the north of Connemara.

THE CELTIC INHERITANCE: IRISH FOLKLORE

Wherever you go in Ireland it is almost impossible not to encounter the island's enormously rich and pervasive folk heritage. Climb a hill, study some geographical feature, or even a natural object like a tree, or stand beside a lake or in front of a ruined castle, church or monastery, and there will be someone around to tell you of the things that may – or may not – have happened here in the often far distant past.

You might be told, for instance, that the Giant's Causeway in County Antrim was made by the mighty hero Finn MacCool to provide himself with stepping stones to Scotland; or that Tory Island, off the Donegal coast, was once the home of Balor of the Evil Eye, leader of a race of sea pirates called the Fomhoire; or that the tragic children of the King of Lir spent 300 of the 900 years they were condemned to exist as swans on Inishglora, off the coast of Mayo, and yet another 300 on Lough Derravaragh in County Westmeath.

All of these stories first gained currency many centuries ago and grew out of the fact that the Celts (or Gaels), coming to Ireland from Europe in the early Stone Age period (around the third century BC), brought with them a strong story-telling tradition but no written language. Their history was passed down the generations by word of mouth and their priests, the Druids, spent many years of their training committing the stories to memory so that they would be preserved forever. Alongside the history and story-telling aspect

OPPOSITE: The Hill of Tara, rising gently out of the plains of County Meath, has occupied a special place in Irish history and folklore for nearly 5,000 years.

LEFT: Navan Fort (Emain Macha), County Armagh, was built by Queen Macha and, it is believed, became the capital of ancient Ulster and the seat of its kings for 600 years.

THE WEST

OPPOSITE: The 'Giant's Organ' on the Giant's Causeway in County Antrim has long been associated with stories of the hero Finn MacCool.

of Celtic culture ran a strong supernatural vein, growing out of the Celts' belief in many gods and their conviction that certain aspects of their natural surroundings – trees, rivers, and springs – were sacred. Thus, their lore was full of these themes, which expressed itself in stories of fairies, leprechauns and banshees.

Christianity, reaching Ireland in the fifth century, had a rapid effect on Irish folklore, for there soon began a great interplay between the oral traditions of the Celts and the written traditions of the Christian monks. The vernacular literature of Ireland, the oldest in Europe, can be dated from about the sixth century, when the tales of pre-Christian Celtic folklore, many of them no doubt altered to fit the Christian ethic under which the people now lived, began to be written down. Because the Celts were a warrior race, their tales were full of the doings of heroes and warriors.

Cúchullain (the Hound of Ulster) was the most famous warrior in Irish folklore, who began his heroic life by killing the savage hound of Culainn the Smith when he was only seven. Cúchullain is supposed to have used a hurling stick as his weapon, thus indicating the ancient Gaelic origins of the popular sport. Then there was Finn MacCool (or Fionn Mac Cumhaill), a great warrior of the time of King Cormac Mac Airt, said to have reigned at Tara in the third century. Finn, from his fortress on the Hill of Allen in County Kildare, led his band of hunter-warriors, the Fianna troop, and his great hound Bran, into many heroic exploits.

Scholars have grouped the ancient Irish sagas into four cycles. The first, the Mythological Cycle, includes stories about the people who lived in Ireland before the Celts, and includes the story of the Battle of Moytura and the famous tale of the Children of Lir. This is a 'wicked stepmother' story, the stepmother being the second wife of the King of Lir, who was so jealous of the king's children that she turned them into swans, condemned to live as such for 900 years. So potent is this story that, even today, it is illegal to kill a swan in Ireland.

Cúchulainn was the leading character in what is now called the Ulster Cycle, which recounts the deeds of the Red Branch Knights. Navan Fort, near Armagh, is believed to be the remains of the fort and settlement called Emain Macha, capital of ancient Ulster, which features in the Cycle; one of its best-known stories, 'The Cattle Raid of Cooley', was one of the earliest tales of Irish folklore to be written down.

The exploits of Finn MacCool and the Fianna are the basis of the Ossianic Cycle, sometimes called the Fenian Cycle. Ossian (or Oisin) was Finn's son and a poet as well as a warrior. Ossian chose to enter Tir na nOg, the 'Land of Eternal Youth', to be with the beautiful Niamh of the Golden Hair. After 300 years spent there, he yearned to return home, which he eventually did after numerous exploits. Back in Ireland he met St. Patrick and recounted to the saint all the stories he knew about his father, the Fianna, and Tir na nOg: hence the Ossian Cycle.

The fourth group of sagas, the Historical Cycle, or the Cycle of Kings, tells stories of the kings of Ireland and is probably part history and part fiction.

The deeds and actions of the early saints in Ireland have also contributed to the country's rich store of folklore. Many tales are told of the miraculous doings of the saints, which are easy to dismiss as myth or legend until someone comes along to demonstrate that they might indeed be true, as did Tim Severin, when he successfully retraced the sea route St. Brendan is said to have taken across the Atlantic to North America.

The fact that folklore lives on in Ireland today is largely due to the revival of interest in the island's Gaelic past in the 19th century. The Gaelic League, a non-sectarian and non-political organization was set up in 1893 with the declared aim of reviving the Gaelic language and returning to Ireland's cultural roots. Government support, after the establishment of the Irish Free State, ensured that the speaking of Gaelic was seen as a matter of national pride, and remains so today. However, a knowledge of Gaelic is not essential for anyone wishing to read the stories of old Ireland, for new versions of the tales are published regularly in English.

CHAPTER SEVEN
THE NORTH-WEST
Donegal, Sligo, Leitrim

*BELOW: The sea pink (*Armeria maritima*) growing on the foreshore near Malin Head on the Inishowen peninsula, County Donegal.*

For many centuries there was little to link the three counties of Ireland's north-west corner. Geographically, Donegal's wild inland mountain country, its dramatic coastline of towering, precipitous cliffs, skirted by golden beaches, with wind-torn spits of land jutting out into the Atlantic, is regarded as very different from the quieter rural charms of Sligo and Leitrim. Historically

OPPOSITE RIGHT: The west face of the Celtic Christian High Cross in the graveyard of St. Columba's Church at Drumcliff, County Sligo.

LEFT: The River Drowes forms a gently flowing dividing line between the counties of Leitrim and Donegal near Bundoran. Beyond is the range of the Dartry Mountains.

BELOW: Intricate carving on a grave slab at St. Columba's in Drumcliff.

*FAR RIGHT: The yellow iris (*Iris pseudacorusis*) is a common sight in marshy areas throughout Ireland.*

there was a great difference, too, in that Donegal was a county of the province of Ulster, whereas Sligo, a county with an ancient tradition of Celtic history and myth, together with Leitrim, were within the province of Connaught.

Partition in 1921 wrought a change, however, when all three counties became part of the Republic. Despite its historical

closeness to the other counties of Ulster and the fact that the county had always looked to Derry (Londonderry) as its main city, Catholic-dominated Donegal seemed an uneasy bedfellow for the new Northern Ireland with its Protestant majority.

Donegal is still something of a county apart, in today's Ireland, whose golden beaches still look as if they have never known holiday crowds, despite the numerous small seaside resorts that dot the coast. Inland, much of the centre of the county is

LEFT: Doe Castle on the Sheep Haven shore near Creeslough, once a stronghold of the Scots MacSweeney clan allied with the O'Donnells.

*BELOW: Ivy-leaved toadflax (*Cymbalaria muralis*), that grows in walls throughout Ireland.*

OPPOSITE: View from the bridge at Carrick-on-Shannon, Leitrim, where fishing and crusing are popular pastimes on the Shannon inland waterway.

LEFT: Kathy and Roger Adair in the garden of their home at Marble Hill, near Dunfanaghy in north Donegal.

OPPOSITE: The uninhabited offshore island of Inishmurray, County Sligo, where the remains of an early Irish monastic settlement, probably founded by Saint Molaise in the sixth century, can be seen. It has a 13-ft (4-m) high enclosure wall, the site containing various ecclesiastical buildings, including more enclosures, an oratory, two churches, a clochan, a large beehive-shaped cell and other remains, the whole being constructed of what is probably local limestone rubble.

LEFT: Carrowmore, the largest prehistoric cemetery in Ireland, is located south-west of Sligo town, where over 30 tombs, spread out across several fields, make up a huge Stone Age cemetery.

PAGE 254: Glencar Lough spans Counties Sligo and Leitrim.

PAGE 255: Swans and cygnets on Glencar Lough, with the Benbulbin mountain in the distance.

OPPOSITE: The Creevykeel prehistoric court tomb located north of Sligo town. This 4,500-year-old megalith, lying almost at sea level immediately to the east of the main Sligo to Donegal road, has been excavated and the site tidied up.

LEFT: Evening light falls on County Donegal's 2,466-ft (752-m) Errigal Mountain, the tallest peak in the Derryveagh Mountains, with the village of Dunlewy lying in its shadow.

A corner of the flower-filled gardens surrounding Glenveagh Castle in County Donegal.

dominated by mountains bisected by long, narrow glens. To the north, the untamed beauty of the Derryveagh Mountains, dominated by the quartzite cone-shaped peak of Errigal Mountain, adds to Donegal's apparent remoteness from 21st-century life, while to the south, the Blue Stack Mountains can be explored along many miles of scenic routes and mountain walks through glens and valleys by lovely loughs and impressive mountains.

IN DONEGAL'S CENTRAL GLENS

The remoteness of inland Donegal is, in fact, more apparent than real. The finest scenery of the Derryveagh Mountains lies at the heart of what has been for some time an environment-conscious phenomenon – a national park. This one is the Glenveagh National Park, which covers nearly 25,000 acres (10,200 hectares) and includes the beautiful valley of the River Glenveagh, flowing into Lough Beagh, and the marshy valley called the Poisoned Glen, named thus because Balor of the Evil Eye, the Celtic god of darkness, was slain here by Lugh, causing the god's single eye to poison the ground on which it fell. There is a visitor centre in the park from which minibuses transport visitors unwilling or unable to walk through the park's glorious landscape to Glenveagh Castle on the shore of Lough Beagh.

Glenveagh Castle, built of imposing granite in 1870 by John George Adair, infamous for his eviction of the tenants of several small-holdings here during the Great Famine, now belongs to the Irish National Parks Service, having been returned to the people, as it were, by its last owner, the American art dealer Henry

Mcllhenny, in the 1970s. The castle is well worth a visit, not only for its splendid interior but also for its formal gardens.

Another house with plenty to interest in the area is Glebe House, 4 miles (6km) south of the National Park Visitor Centre by road – or three miles by way of a walk over the mountain bog tops, for Glebe House overlooks Gartan Lough, in the next valley east from Glenveagh Park. Glebe, a Regency house, is also set in beautiful gardens, but these are generally of less interest to visitors than the fine paintings housed in the purpose-built gallery. Glebe House was home to the English-born painter and art collector, Derek Hill, and his collection includes paintings by the Tory Island Primitives and by Renoir, Degas, Picasso, Kokoschka, Braque and several other Irish artists, including Jack B. Yeats.

Further down Gartan Lough's southern shore is the Colmcille Heritage Centre, Church Hill, a reminder that St. Columba (*Colmcille* in Irish) was born near here in 521. In the modern building is a finely detailed exhibition featuring the life of the saint and an impressive collection of stained glass. Just off the road from Glenveagh to Gartan Lough is a large cross marking the saint's birthplace and an ancient stone slab, known locally as the Flagstone of Loneliness, upon which Columba is reputed to have slept. In doing so, he imbued the stone with the miraculous power of lightening the burden of sorrows of anyone lying upon it. Archeologists, however, have rather

LEFT, PAGES 260 & 261: The subject of both myth and speculation, the Grianán of Aileach is a ring fort, possibly dating from around 1000 AD, that was built on the site of an ancient hill fort said to have been the work of Dagda, a king of the Tuatha De Danann, in 1700 BC on top of Greenan Mountain in County Donegal. The Grianán of Aileach is noted on Ptolomy's map of 140 AD, and it was the residence of the O'Neills, High Kings of Ireland in the fifth century, and later the seat of the O'Donnells, chieftains of Donegal. It is thought to have been a place of sun worship in prehistoric times, or of the hibernation of Gráinne, a Celtic sun-goddess.

OPPOSITE: St. Aengus's Roman Catholic Church at Burt, designed by Donegal architect, Liam McCormack, was inspired by the nearby Grianán of Aileach.

LEFT & PAGE 264: Killybegs, Ireland's largest fishing port, is a natural deepwater harbour in Donegal, home to many of the largest Irish-registered fishing trawlers. It also handles many other types of shipping, including passenger cruise liners and container vessels.

PAGE 265: The countryside around Killybegs to the south of County Donegal.

disappointingly declared the stone to be part of a Bronze Age gallery tomb, which did nothing to deter people, during the harrowing period of mass emigration, from coming here the night before their departure in the hope of alleviating their despair at leaving home.

The largest town of Donegal's central region, and a good point from which to tour, is bustling Letterkenny. Although the county town is Lifford, to the south-east, it is Letterkenny, set on the River Swilly just above the spot where the river flows into Lough Swilly, that features in the guidebooks as Donegal's main commercial centre. The town's long main street is dominated by the 19th-century Gothic-style St. Eunan's Cathedral with its imposing steeple. There is also an interesting County Museum, housed in a recently restored workhouse. Letterkenny prides itself on its entertainment facilities, which include plenty of typically Irish bars, several of which offer Irish music; numerous nightclubs, including one of the largest in Ireland; and a good cinema centre. The town holds an International Folk Festival each August.

St. Columba has a connection of sorts with the area round Letterkenny, as with so many other places in Donegal. It was here that he eventually killed the man-eating monster known as the Swilly (or *Suileach*, in Irish), although the saint still had to contend with the various pieces into which he had cut the monster, all of which continued to attack him.

OPPOSITE: The view south-west down the Owenea river near Ardara.

LEFT: The mountain road through the magnificent Glengesh Pass, one of the most spectacular sights in Donegal, on its way to Ardara, a centre for tweed-weaving and knitwear production..

PAGE 268: Fishing boats on Lough Meela, that lies between Dungloe and Burtonport in west Donegal.

PAGE 269: The peaceful and unspoilt beach at Culdaff on the Inishowen peninsula in north Donegal.

OPPOSITE: The Bracky river weaves through Maghera Strand to Loughros Beg Bay.

LEFT: Looking north-east down the valley of the Owenwee river to Loughros Beg Bay, near Ardara, south-west Donegal.

RIGHT & BELOW: The design of Carndonagh village centre, Inishowen, by Gary Doherty, is based on its Celtic Donough Cross.

OPPOSITE: A ruined cottage on the mountain road south-east of Dungloe in west Donegal.

AROUND DONEGAL'S DRAMATIC COAST

Broad Lough Swilly is a sea lough that divides the Inishowen peninsula, Donegal's most northerly and most easterly point, from the Fanad peninsula to the west. Inishowen is the largest of Donegal's peninsulas, though it is not so large that a leisurely tour around it by car cannot be fitted into a day. There are, however, many places which deserve a closer look rather than a cursory glance from a passing car.

OPPOSITE: Looking south over the village of Dunfanaghy toward Muckish Mountain in north Donegal.

LEFT: An old farmstead on the mountain road south-east of Dungloe.

There is Malin Head, for instance, at the peninsula's northern tip; who, having listened to all those radio shipping forecasts, with their romantic-sounding names, could drive past this, Ireland's most northerly point, without stopping to look out over the Atlantic, perhaps even to glimpse a fishing boat pushing out to sea from one of the numerous villages and ports around the coast? The tower on the cliff here was originally built in 1805 by the British Admiralty to monitor shipping, and was later used as a signal tower by Lloyd's of London.

In great contrast to Malin Head and its tower is Donegal's most ancient monument, the circular stone fort, Grianán of Aileach (pages 259–261), at the southern end of the peninsula 6 miles (10km) west of Letterkenny. The site is probably prehistoric, when it was thought to have been a place of pagan worship. Later, it became a Christian site and St. Patrick is said to have baptized the founder of the O'Neill dynasty here in 450.

The northern coast of Donegal stretches westwards in a series of headlands, among the most scenic of which is Horn Head, rising 600ft (180m) straight out of the Atlantic and offering a haven for a rich variety of birdlife. The coast turns south at Bloody Foreland, so-called because the rocks of the headland glow ruby-red at sunset. Out to sea, between Horn Head and Bloody Foreland is Tory Island, separated from the north-west corner of Donegal by the turbulent Tory Channel and accessible by boat from Gortahork, daily in summer and weather permitting in winter.

OPPOSITE & LEFT: Near Glencolumbcille, Donegal. Here peat (turf) has been cut and stacked to dry so that it can provide fuel for winter hearths.

OPPOSITE & LEFT:
Glencolumbcille, named for St.
Columba, is one of the devotional
sites on the annual pilgrimage
around the valley.

PAGE 280: Looking to the south-
east from Falcarragh to the
Derryveagh Mountains.

PAGE 281: Glen Head rises above
the road from Glencolumbcille to
Malin Beg.

Tory Island has its place in Celtic mythology as the home of Balor of the Evil Eye, and the islanders maintain a Celtic tradition by speaking Gaelic and having their own monarch even today. They have also developed, in recent years, their own school of primitive artists, inspired by a local man, James Dixon, who felt he could do better work than the visiting English painter, Derek Hill (of Glebe House); a gallery on the island now exists to show their work.

This northern part of Donegal, centred on Gortahork but stretching from Fanad Head round the west coast down to the 1,972-ft (601-m) Slieve League, whose south face rises sheer out of the sea on the northern shore of Donegal Bay, is one of Ireland's regions of *Gaeltacht*, which, at its southern extremity, comes face to face with modern tourism, for Donegal Bay is a holiday mecca for thousands of people every summer, and Bundoran, on the bay's southern shore, is one of Ireland's liveliest seaside resorts, full of amusement arcades, aquaworlds, souvenir shops and bright lights. Great fun in itself, Bundoran is so different from the country north of Donegal Bay, which could be said to be contained in a world of its own.

Lying almost in the shadow of Slieve League is the village of Glencolumbcille (the 'Glen of Saint Colmcille') and its nearby Folk Village Museum, a recreation of Donegal rural life through the ages. Glencolumbcille's remote, rugged setting at the head of Glen Bay seems the perfect place to have built a retreat for prayer

OPPOSITE: The fishing port of Greencastle on the Inishhowen shore of Lough Foyle in north Donegal.

LEFT: One of several memorial plaques at Greencastle, dedicated to Inishowen sailors lost at sea.

RIGHT: Father and son Mickey and Shaun Rodgers in Bonner's Pub near Kincaslough, west Donegal.

RIGHT: Father and son Mickey and Shaun Rodgers in Bonner's Pub near Kincaslough, west Donegal.

OPPOSITE: The coast near Kincaslough.

and contemplation and one can see why St. Columba should have chosen it. It is still a place of pilgrimage, and pilgrims make a penitential walk around the glen in the early hours of the morning of 9 June, the saint's feast day, stopping to pray at the Stations of the Cross which are marked by boulders, cairns and even pagan standing stones.

More taxing by far than this midsummer pilgrimage is Donegal's other famous religious event, at Station Island in

RIGHT: A roadside shrine to the Virgin Mary, Loughros Beg Bay.

FAR RIGHT: Statue of St. Patrick on the shore of Lough Derg.

OPPOSITE: Station Island in Lough Derg houses the cave known as St. Patrick's Purgatory, a major place of pilgrimage since the Middle Ages.

Lough Derg, south-east of Donegal town, where the desire to partake in an extremely rigorous three-day retreat, St. Patrick's Purgatory, has attracted pilgrims since at least the 12th century.

IN COUNTY LEITRIM

Both Sligo and Leitrim stretch to the southern shores of Donegal Bay, though their hold on it is rather more tenuous than Donegal's. There is a feeling that, once you have travelled down the narrow strip that connects Donegal to the rest of the Republic, you have come to a quieter, more unobtrusive part of the country. Indeed, if you stick to the coast road from Bundoran, it is possible to pass through Leitrim and into Sligo almost without noticing.

Leitrim's two-mile coastline has only one town, Tullaghan, one of Ireland's less exciting resorts, though the Drowes and Duff rivers, which flow into the sea on either side of the village, offer excellent salmon fishing. The 1,000-year-old High Cross, which stands on a mound nearby, was not always there: it was found in the sea in the 18th century, having probably come from a monastery that once stood on the shore near the mouth of the River Drowes.

Travel a little way inland from Leitrim's coast and you are in a more interesting landscape, where deep valleys, such as Glencar and Glenade, cutting through the surprisingly rugged mountains, offer fine walking, its rivers attracting fishermen eager to do battle with salmon and other freshwater fish. Centuries ago, the battles

OPPOSITE: The tidal beach leading to Cruit Island, west Donegal.

*LEFT: Sea kale (*Crambe maritima*) grows on maritime shingle or sandy beaches throughout Ireland.*

*RIGHT: White campion (*Silene alba*), growing at Kincaslough, Donegal.*

OPPOSITE: Looking north-east over the estuary of the Gweebarra river near Maas in west Donegal.

RIGHT: Storm waves batter the coast near Malin Head at the northernmost tip of Ireland.

OPPOSITE: Landscape at Culdaff on the Inishowen peninsula.

RIGHT & OPPOSITE: Two views of Silver Strand, south of Glencolumbcille.

PAGE 296: Looking east from Malin Head, the northernmost tip of Ireland.

PAGE 297: Walking the cliff road to Slieve League with Benbulbin mountain, County Sligo, in the distance.

were far bloodier, in that they involved the warriors of numerous local chiefs.

Dromahair, almost on the border with Sligo near Lough Gill, first found a place in history in the fifth century as the home of St. Patrick for 17 years, the saint founding a church, a monastery and a nunnery in this quiet place on the River Bonet. Seven centuries later, Dromahair, by now a seat of the powerful O'Rourke family, was again thrust into the forefront of Irish history when Dervorgilla, wife of Tieran O'Rourke, Prince of Breifne, was abducted by Dermot MacMurrough, King of Leinster. Eventually the abduction cost MacMurrough his throne, causing him to appeal to Henry II of England for help in getting it back, with the result that the Anglo-Normans marched into Irish history.

Much of the rest of Leitrim is dominated by loughs and rivers. The Shannon, flowing through spectacular Lough Allen, which virtually divides the county in two, is just one of many rivers and waterways, including the Ballinamore-Ballyconnell Canal, which make south Leitrim a fisherman's paradise. Here, the high plateau, falling away to the hillocks of the drumlin country round Mohill, is a good place for ramblers and walkers on land and for cruising holidaymakers on water.

One of the north-west's most popular centres for coarse fishing and for cruising holidays is Leitrim's county town, Carrick-on-Shannon, set on a broad stretch of the Shannon below Lough Key. Apart from its fine lock and other waterworks, built early in the 19th century when Carrick was an important town on Ireland's water transport system, the small town's main point of interest is its possession of Ireland's smallest church, the Costello Memorial Chapel. This tiny place, crammed between two buildings, was built in 1877 by a local merchant, Edward Costello, as a memorial and burial place for his young wife, Josephine. The Costellos now lie in the chapel, buried in lead coffins protected by thick slabs of glass.

OPPOSITE & BELOW: The dramatic cliffs at Slieve League are among some of the highest in Europe.

RIGHT: Patsy Dan Rogers, painter and 'King' of Tory Island.

OPPOSITE: The lighthouse in the bleak north corner of Tory Island, off the north-west Donegal coast.

RIGHT: William Butler Yeats, photographed when he was about 40.

OPPOSITE: Trotting horses, returning from Ballinasloe Fair, quench their thirst in the river by Ballylee Castle, near Gort, Galway, once the summer home of the poet W.B. Yeats.

IN THE LAND OF WILLIAM BUTLER YEATS

Geologists tell us that much of County Sligo was carved out by Ice-Age glaciers, leaving in the south the lovely valleys and glittering lakes that make this landscape one of the finest in Connaught. Further north, the country, marked by more lakes but dominated by limestone outcrops, of which Benbulbin is the most striking, has been made that much lovelier in the minds of men by the poetry of William Butler Yeats.

County Sligo was not Yeats's home county: he was born in Dublin, was educated there and in London, and spent half his life outside Ireland. But his deep love of Irish culture and the country of the north-west, immortalized in some of his finest poetry, forever links him with County Sligo.

Having spent many of the happiest days of his childhood there, he recalled, years later, visiting the pretty resort of Rosses Point at the entrance to Sligo Bay at Glencar Lough, and Lough Gill and its tiny Isle of Innisfree, where 'midnight's all a glimmer, and noon a purple glow', to quote one of his best-known poems, 'The Lake Isle of Innisfree'. Yeats's family had many connections with Sligo, the largest town in the north-west after Derry, and although Yeats himself owned a home in County Galway, near his friend Lady Gregory's house at Coole Park, it was the village of Drumcliff, near Sligo, that Yeats chose as his burial place 'under bare Ben Bulben's head'.

Yeats died in the south of France in 1939 and it was not until 1948 that his body was brought back to Ireland to be buried in the

Protestant churchyard in Drumcliff. Today, Drumcliff is one of the highlights of regularly planned tours of the 'Yeats Country', which attract many thousands of visitors to Sligo.

While Yeats may have become one of Sligo's greatest tourist attractions, he is not its only one. Yeats loved Sligo as much for its splendid culture, packed full of historical incident and myth, as for the beauty of its countryside, and these same things continue to attract people today.

For those interested in Ireland's ancient past, County Sligo holds a special fascination. At the Carrowmore Megalithic Cemetery (page 253), south of Sligo, can be seen tombs at least 700 years older than the famous ones at Newgrange in County Meath. Carrowmore is the second largest megalithic tomb site in Europe, with only Carnac in France exceeding it in size. Then there are the passage tombs at Carrowkeel, high in the Bricklieve Mountains in the south of the county. Here, passage graves, set in limestone cairns, date from 2500–2000 BC. One of the roofed tombs, the cruciform-shaped Cairn K, can be entered, when a spine-tingling step into the distant past is usually experienced.

For those whose interest lies in more recent history, an evocative trip can be made to the island of Innishmurray (see page 252), 4 miles (6km) off Sligo's northern coast, where St. Molaise founded a monastery in the sixth century. The Vikings destroyed much of it, but there are still three churches to be seen, and there is a beehive hut which was once a school. About 50 stone memorials are scattered over the island, at which pilgrims performed the Stations of the Cross until as recently as 1948.

A trip of a different kind is the hike many people make up the south-eastern flank of Knocknarea, the 'Hill of the Kings', west of Sligo town. At the hill's summit is a 5,000-year-old passage tomb, popularly believed to be the burial place of the legendary Maeve, Queen of Connaught, one of the great characters of Celtic mythology.

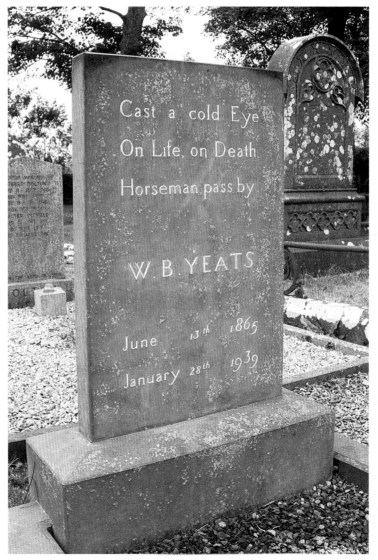

OPPOSITE: Tranquil Lough Gill, with the Dartry Mountains beyond, was one of Yeats's favourite places. Would he have heard the silvery sound of the bell from the Dominican Abbey in Sligo, which is said to be at the bottom of the lake? According to a legend associated with the lake, only those without sin are able to hear it.

FAR LEFT: The interior of Drumcliff's St. Columba's Church, where Yeats is buried, was also where his great-grandfather was once the rector.

LEFT: Headstone of Yeats's tomb in the Protestant churchyard at Drumcliff in Co. Sligo. The poet wrote his own epitaph.

CHAPTER EIGHT

NORTHERN IRELAND

Antrim, Armagh, Down, Fermanagh
Derry, Tyrone

BELOW: Armagh has two cathedrals named after Saint Patrick: this is the Church of Ireland's St. Patrick's, seat of the Protestant Archbiship of Armagh.

FAR RIGHT: Gazing at the world out of the distant past, this Celtic head in Armagh Cathedral dates from the Iron Age.

Six of the nine counties of the ancient province of Ulster became part of the United Kingdom as the Province of Northern Ireland under the Anglo-Irish Treaty of 1921. Of the six counties, Armagh is the smallest and Tyrone the least populated; Antrim boasts the Province's main tourist attractions, including the Giant's Causeway and the lovely Glens of Antrim, while Fermanagh, the only one of the six that cannot claim a share of vast Lough Neagh's shoreline, is the lake district of Ireland, with a third of its area under stretches of water which include the lovely Upper and Lower Lough Ernes. County Derry

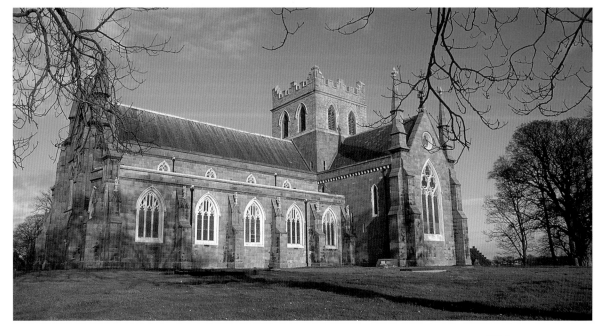

and County Down are both steeped in history and endowed with much fine scenery.

Today, despite more than 30 years of the 'Troubles', as the Irish refer with remarkable sangfroid to the hideous carnage of bombings and shootings that has polarized society north of the border, life in the six counties is good and the country itself remains as lovely and as accessible as it has always been. Recent

LEFT: Looking north-west over Lower Lough Erne from the Cliffs of Magho, Fermanagh, towards Donegal.

PAGE 308: Queen's University of Belfast, established in 1845: the Gothic façade of the Lanyon Building, designed by the Belfast architect Sir Charles Lanyon.

PAGE 309: The Palm House in Belfast's Botanic Gardens, one of the earliest examples of a curvilinear and cast-iron glasshouse. Begun in the 1830s, the two wings were completed in 1840 by Richard Turner of Dublin, who later built the Great Palm House at Kew Gardens in England.

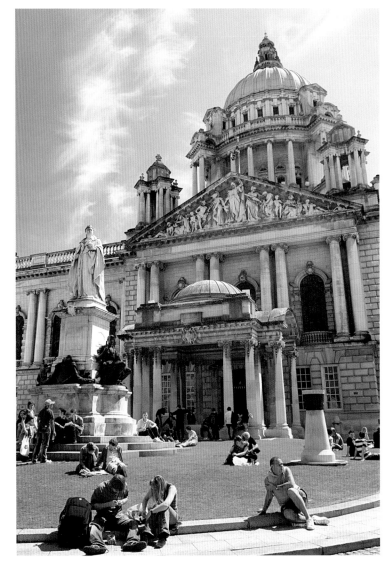

OPPOSITE: Two views of the magnificent Belfast City Hall. Designed by Alfred Brumwell Thomas and built in Portland stone, it was completed in 1906, its purpose being to reflect Belfast City's new status, granted by Queen Victoria in 1888. It is the home of Belfast City Council.

LEFT: The 'Big Fish' sculpture, by John Kindness, stands on Donegall Quay, Belfast, in the centre of the docklands redevelopment area. It was commissioned to celebrate the regeneration of the Belfast docks and to mark the return of salmon to the River Lagan.

BELOW: Samson and Goliath are Harland & Wolff's twin shipbuilding gantry cranes, situated on Queen's Island, Belfast, where the tragic RMS Titanic *was built.*

FAR RIGHT: A vintage postcard comparing Titanic *and her sister ship* Oympic *with some of the world's then tallest buildings.*

co-operation between the Province and the Republic in restoring the Ballinamore-Ballyconnell Canal, linking the River Shannon with the lakes and rivers of Fermanagh, has helped to make the lovely country around the canal and river system accessible to many more people, with holidaymakers, on pleasure boats and cruisers, able to enjoy much more of the serene beauty which surrounds them.

In Northern Ireland, a new feeling of optimism was in evidence as the Millennium approached, despite the long progress

SURPASSING THE GREATEST BUILDINGS AND MEMORIALS OF EARTH

The White Star Line's New Triple-screw Steamers
"OLYMPIC" ☆ "TITANIC"
LARGEST AND FINEST IN THE WORLD

towards peace, which was an optimism well-expressed in the Province's considerable programme of rebuilding. Many attractive modern buildings went up on bombed and derelict sites, one of the finest of these, and perhaps one that best expressed the new spirit abroad in Northern Ireland, being Belfast's Waterfront Hall, described as 'a fresh, Modernist take on the Albert Hall', which was opened early in 1997.

This splendid concert hall, with its glittering, curved-glass façade, stands on the bank of the River Lagan in a part of the city where the skyline has been dominated for many years by the great cranes of the Harland and Wolff Shipyard. Near the Waterfront Hall, there is a hotel (one of an international chain), numerous office buildings, new shops and multi-storey car parks.

Vintage steam-powered cranes, survivors from the days when Titanic *was under construction. Launched on 31 May 1911,* Titanic *was 882ft 9in (269m) long and 92ft 6in (28m) at the beam, with a Gross Register Tonnage of 46,328 tons and a height of 60ft (18m) from the waterline to the boat deck. She struck an iceberg on 14 April 1912, when making her maiden voyage to New York, and sank the next day with great loss of life.*

OPPOSITE: The Grand Opera House, Great Victoria Street, is a late Victorian design by Frank Matcham. It is also Belfast's main theatre venue.

LEFT: The Crown Bar on Great Victoria Street, one of the city's most popular landmarks.

PAGE 316: The Custom House on Custom House Square, Donegall Quay.

PAGE 317 LEFT: The Albert Memorial Clock in Queen's Square, completed to the design of W.J. Barre in 1853.

PAGE 317 RIGHT: Interior of the Parish Church of St. George, a Church of Ireland foundation located on High Street in Belfast City Centre. It has a strong musical tradition and is the only Anglo-Catholic parish in Northern Ireland.

On 8 May 2007, with Britain having ruled Northern Ireland from London for the last five years, during which time sectarian violence had been much reduced, the Protestants and Catholics of Northern Ireland regained local control of their Province. But will this power-sharing agreement last or will the decades-long Troubles return? Only time will tell.

BELFAST TODAY

There was a time, in the 19th century, when Belfast's growth far outstripped that of Dublin, for the great industrial expansion of Victorian England spread across the Irish Sea to Belfast rather than to Dublin, and Belfast became one of the world's major engineering and shipbuilding centres as well as an important manufacturer of rope and linen, the latter industry having been founded in the 17th century by French Huguenots.

There are many signs of Belfast's 19th-century prosperity still to be seen in the city today, from the imposing and splendidly domed City Hall in Donegall Square and the neo-Romanesque St. Anne's Anglican Cathedral in Donegall Street to the Grand Opera House, nicknamed by Belfast 'the eastern palace' on account of the onion domes atop its façade. Belfast's well-known Linen Hall Library, also in Donegall Square, no longer has any connection with Northern Ireland's important linen-weaving industry. The White Linen Hall, in which it is housed, was established as a library in 1788 and now has the best collection in

A Simmental cow suckling a Belgian Blue calf on the banks of the River Bush, Country Antrim.

existence of early books printed in Belfast. It is here that you can study the huge number of works on political life in Northern Ireland published since 1966.

A gentle 15-minute stroll from Donegall Square, the hub of Belfast from which most of the city's main streets radiate, leads to another grand example of 19th-century architecture, still fulfilling an important role in this the new century. This is the main

FAR LEFT: An ancient Celtic Christian round tower in the town of Antrim.

BELOW: Robert Boyce, one of the regular musicians to appear at the Fullerton Arms near to the village of Ballintoy in Antrim.

OPPOSITE: The basalt and limestone landscape surrounding Balintoy harbour, on the scenic North Antrim Coast Road between Ballycastle and the Giant's Causeway.

LEFT: Ballycastle beach, looking towards the foreland of Fair Head, with the west coast of Scotland in the far distance. Ballycastle lies at the heart of the Causeway Coast and Glens of Antrim.

BELOW: The annual agricultural show in Ballymoney, Antrim: prize-winners in the livestock parade.

RIGHT: The ruins of the Franciscan friary at Bonamargy, founded by Rory MacQuillan in 1500 in the town of Ballycastle on the north Antrim coast.

building of Queen's University, Northern Ireland's most prestigious seat of learning, which attracts students from many parts of the world.

Opposite the Grand Opera House in Great Victoria Street is an unforgettable Victorian 'gin palace', the Crown Bar (page 315), exuberantly decorated with tiles and stained glass, carved oak and gaslights. It belongs to the National Trust, a body which has many of the finest buildings and most precious tracts of

countryside in Northern Ireland within its careful guardianship. The National Trust, in preserving these different aspects of the Province's heritage, is working along appropriate lines, for throughout Northern Ireland the many intertwining strands of the Province's history can be best understood against the background of its fine scenery.

WHERE HISTORY AND COUNTRYSIDE MERGE

A visit to Navan Fort, in the heart of quietly rural County Armagh, for instance, where the great circular enclosure with its man-made central mound can be explored, and you are transported back to the mists of Celtic myth and ancient Irish

history. This place, once called Eamain Macha, was the capital from which Celtic kings and queens ruled ancient Ulster. In use as long ago as 2000 BC, the site was most actively occupied in the century before Christ. The great folk hero, Cúchullain, the Hound of Ulster, is associated with the place, as are the mythical Red Branch Knights.

FAR LEFT: Old wrought-iron estate gates at Ballylough House, near Bushmills, County Antrim.

ABOVE: Ryan Smith cutting silage near Castle Cat, Antrim.

Cúchullain's exploits, celebrated in myth and legend, also emphasize the separation in history of Ulster from the other provinces of Ireland: there has always been a border of sorts between the people of Ulster and those of the other ancient provinces of Ireland.

Eamain Macha was founded by Queen Macha, celebrated in mythology as the Celtic war-fertility goddess who also gave her name to Armagh (*Ard Mhacha* means 'Macha's Height'), the county town and one of Ireland's oldest cities just two miles (or a quick cycle ride in this fine cycling country) to the east of Navan

OPPOSITE: Mares and foals pastured at Ballylough, Bushmills.

FAR LEFT: An international motorcycle road race champion in August 1964, Richard Creith is pictured with his 500-cc Manx Norton at his farm in Ballylough, Bushmills.

BELOW LEFT: Wool clippers secure a farmyard door.

BELOW: Ian McCollum spinning for salmon on the River Bush in north Antrim.

FAR RIGHT: Hand-tied trout and salmon fly-fishing ties.

Fort. This small, quietly handsome town, is at the heart of Irish Christianity, for St. Patrick founded two churches here in the fifth century. Today, Armagh is the ecclesiastical capital of Catholic Ireland, with its heart in St. Patrick's Cathedral. The city is also the seat of the Anglican Primacy in Ireland, centred on the Church of Ireland cathedral, built on the site of St. Patrick's second church.

LEFT: A female donkey with her week-old foal, County Antrim.

PAGE 328: The Carrick-a-Rede, a rope bridge in north Antrim, believed to have been erected by fishermen to span a deep chasm that enabled them to check their salmon nets. Today it is the challenge of tackling the rope bridge for themselves that attracts visitors.

PAGE 329: The magnificent Carrickfergus Castle in County Antrim was started by John de Courcy, conqueror of Ulster, between c.1180 and his fall in 1204. It was captured by King John after a siege in 1210, and the Middle Ward may date from after that event. The Outer Ward was probably added during Hugh de Lacy's lordship, between 1228 and 1242.

OPPOSITE: The massive four-storey keep at the heart of the Anglo-Norman Dundrum Castle, County Down, stands on the top of a rocky hill commanding fine views south over Dundrum Bay and the Mourne Mountains.

LEFT: The ruins of a castle built on the motte of an earlier Norman motte-and-bailey castle in the village of Clough, County Down. It was probably built during or before the reign of King John (1199–1216), although little else is known of its history.

PAGE 332: The current building on this ancient site is the Victorian Killadeas Church of Ireland Priory Church on the north shore of Lower Loch Erne in Fermanagh.

PAGE 333: Details of the Bishop's Stone in Killadeas's churchyard. On the narrow front edge is a carved head and there is a figure holding a bell and crozier on its broader side.

BELOW: The venting towers and warehouses of Antrim's Old Bushmills Distillery, the world's oldest, established in 1608.

FAR RIGHT: Old Bushmills poster.

St. Patrick himself first landed in Ireland as a missionary at Strangford Lough on the coast of County Down in AD 432. He built his first church at nearby Saul, sailing up the little River Slaney from the lough. There is a memorial chapel and Celtic-style round tower there now, built in the 1930s to commemorate Ireland's most ancient ecclesiastical site. St. Patrick's church is

long gone, of course, as is the monastery built by St. Malachy in the 12th century.

St. Patrick's remains are in Downpatrick, the capital of County Down, probably buried beneath the cathedral, an early 19th-century building on a site which had known many churches over the centuries. Built where several river valleys meet, Downpatrick, not surprisingly, endured many destructive invasions over the centuries, but it also, during and after the period of the Jacobite plantations, attracted many settlers.

Down has witnessed the mingling of political and religious history which has marked Irish life for centuries. After St. Patrick, Christianity spread rapidly throughout Ulster, as it did through

LEFT: *Irish whiskey maturing in oak casks at Old Bushmills Distillery, County Antrim.*

PAGES 336 & 337 LEFT: *The limestone Marble Arch Caves in Cuilcagh Mountain Park, south Fermanagh, were jointly awarded UNESCO Global Geopark status in 2004, one of 25 such sites around the world. This particular cavern is known as the Crystal Palace.*

PAGE 337 RIGHT: *Shamrock, an unofficial symbol of Ireland, is a three-leafed white clover, sometimes referred to as* Trifolium repens, *by others as wood sorrel (*Oxalis acetosella*). It is seen here growing in the limestone pavement below Cuilcagh Mountain.*

*RIGHT: An early purple orchid (*Orchis mascula*), growing in the limestone pavement below Cuilcagh Mountain.*

*FAR RIGHT: Red valerian (*Centranthus ruber*) seeds itself in old walls and on dry banks.*

OPPOSITE: The fuchsia, native to South America, has colonized Ireland to such an extent that it could be considered a native. It commonly forms roadside hedges.

RIGHT: Georgian houses in English Street, in the ancient town of Downpatrick, lead up to Down Cathedral.

OPPOSITE: Pleasure boats on Upper Lough Erne near Enniskillen.

RIGHT: Stained-glass windows in Down Cathedral, showing St. Patrick as a young slave and as a Christian missionary.

OPPOSITE: Visitors to Down Cathedral are told how St. Patrick brought Christianity to Ireland in the fifth century.

PAGE 344 LEFT: Dunluce Castle, fortress of the MacDonnells, chiefs of Antrim, on the coast road near Port Rush, dates from the 13th century.

PAGE 344 RIGHT: A north Antrim farmer, Matt Lyons, in the vestibule of Dunluce Presbyterian Church with his collection box for the new church hall.

PAGE 345: The promontory fort of Dunseverick Castle near Ballycastle in Antrim, in what was once the ancient kingdom of Dalriada, dates from before the time of St. Patrick.

the rest of Ireland. The Anglo-Normans who, unlike the Vikings, remained to settle in the lands they had invaded, managed to maintain an uneasy peace with the Irish chieftains who ruled alongside them. Elizabeth I, fearful that her realm would be invaded by Spain via the back door of Ireland, ended this relatively comfortable co-existence and began the system of

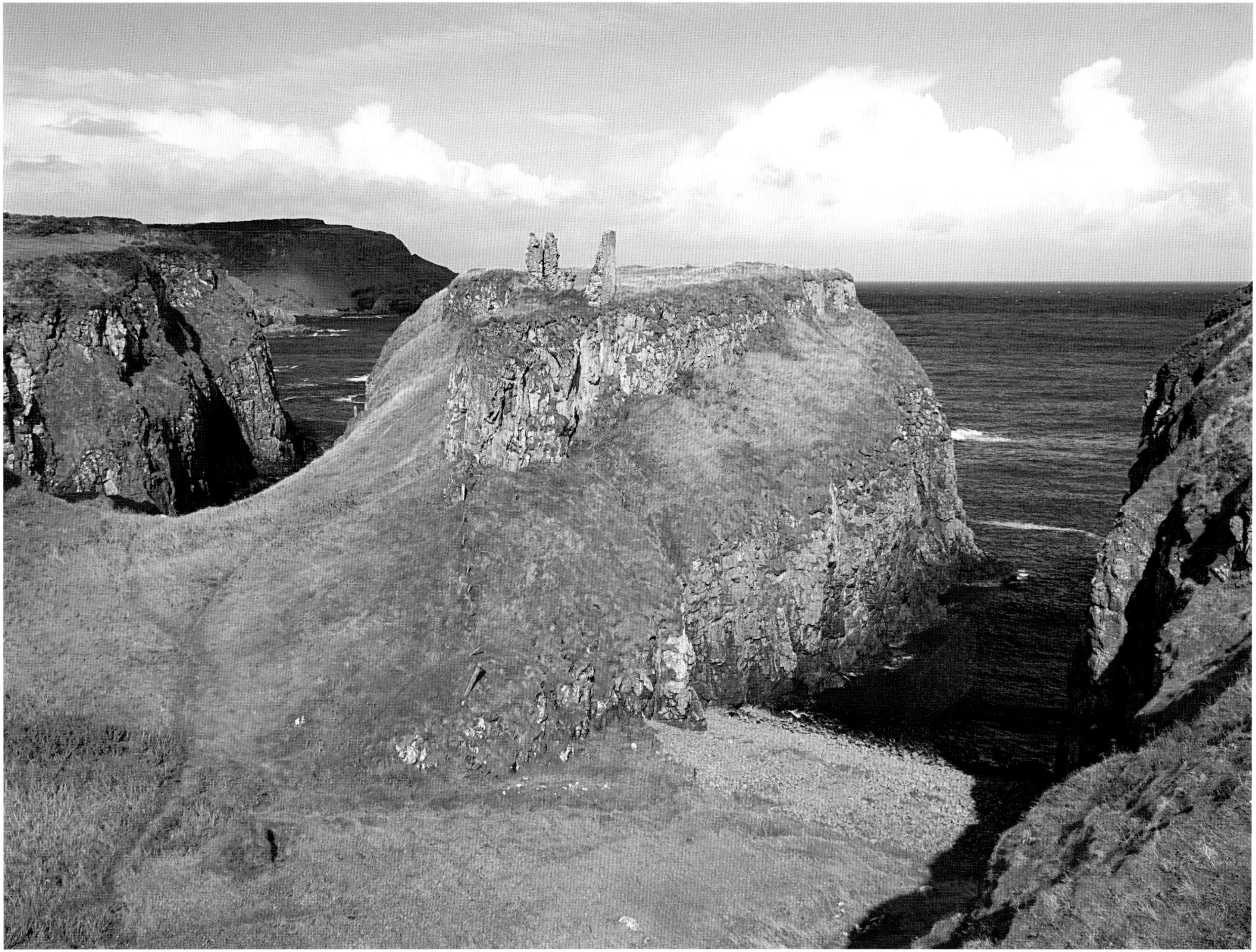

OPPOSITE: Warm evening light casts its glow on the village of Portaferry, County Down.

LEFT: The ferryboat across the narrow entrance to Strangford Lough leaves Portaferry, bound for the village of Strangford.

PAGE 348: The Mourne Mountains: typical drystone walls rise to the craggy summit of Slieve Mountain.

PAGE 349: A vintage pickup tourer travelling the Trassey Road through the Mourne Mountains, with Slieve Bearnagh in the distance.

OPPOSITE: The Victorian Slieve Donard Hotel, Newcastle, beside the world-class Royal County Down golf course.

LEFT: The image of Percy French recalls his song 'The Mountains of Morne', where they sweep down to the sea near Newcastle Promenade.

OPPOSITE: The Giant's Causeway, a collection of about 40,000 interlocking basalt columns resulting from volcanic eruption. Located a little to the north of Bushmills in Antrim, it was declared a UNESCO World Heritage Site in 1986 and a National Nature Reserve in 1987. According to legend, it was a bridge that allowed giants to cross between Ireland and Scotland.

FAR LEFT: The Giant's Organ, one of other unique features from the site.

LEFT & 354–356: The tops of the basalt columns, that form three natural platforms, and have withstood erosion from the pummeling sea, form stepping stones leading from the cliff foot that disappear under the sea.

PAGE 357: A coastal farm landscape near Benbane Head, looking south-east towards Knocklayd Mountain.

RIGHT: The view from Dundrum Castle over the old fishing village and modern apartments of Dundrum Bay, County Down.

OPPOSITE: The important Northern Irish sea-fishing port of Kilkeel, at the southernmost tip of County Down.

sending Protestants from England (especially London) and from Scotland to set up plantations of loyal citizens in Ireland. Her successor, James I (VI of Scotland), continued the policy even more strenuously, which resulted in the infamous 'Flight of the Earls' and the establishment of a Protestant-based rule from which Irish Catholics were excluded.

Among the many towns of Northern Ireland to have been given their present style and shape by this system of plantation are Fermanagh's county town of Enniskillen, set in a narrow spit of land between the Upper and Lower Lough Ernes and

OPPOSITE: A sundial in the beautifully maintained gardens of Glenarm.

LEFT: Glenarm Castle, ancestral home of the earls of Antrim, seen from the walled garden.

BELOW LEFT: An armorial escutcheon in Glenarm's walled garden.

PAGE 362: The ruins of Ardclinis church, near Glenariff, Glens of Antrim, once famous for its silver and bronze medieval treasure. The 12th-century Ardclinis Crozier is now in the National Museum, Dublin.

PAGE 363: Looking north down Glenariff, one of the famous Nine Glens of Antrim and a designated area of outstanding natural beauty.

BELOW: Spring colour comes to the Glendun river in Glendun, one of the Nine Glens of Antrim.

*FAR RIGHT: A burnet rose (*Rosa spinosissima*), growing in the sand dunes of East Strand, Portrush.*

concentrated around the 15th-century Enniskillen Castle and Derry's Coleraine, now a quiet market town and the site of the modern campus of the University of Ulster.

County Derry was particularly heavily planted by Protestant settlers in the 17th century, many of them sent over by City of London companies, which is why the old city of Derry came to be renamed Londonderry. Derry had grown up around a monastery

LEFT: The ancient fortress of Kenbane (Kinbane) Castle, on the north Antrim Coast west of Ballycastle, with Fair Head in the distance.

PAGE 366: An old watermill in the village of Park north of the Sperrin Mountains.

PAGE 367: Looking north from Sawel Mountain, the highest peak in the Sperrin Mountains, towards Limavady and the cliffs above Magilligan.

OPPOSITE: The round tower, one of the finest in Ireland, and monastic buildings of Devenish Island, Fermanagh, seen from the eastern shore of Lower Lough Erne near Enniskillen.

LEFT: Portstewart, Derry, one of the most desirable places in Northern Ireland in which to live. Its long, crescent-shaped seafront promenade, skirting the harbour, is sheltered by rocky headlands, and it was a popular holiday destination for middle-class families in Victorian times.

PAGE 370: The River Rush flows into the Atlantic at Bushfoot, Portballintrae on the Antrim coast.

PAGE 371 ABOVE: The harbour village of Portballintrae.

PAGE 371 BELOW: A narrow-gauge train runs through the sandhills along the old tramway track between Bushmills and the Giant's Causeway.

founded by St. Columba in the sixth century; when the old city was destroyed by fire it was rebuilt by a consortium of City of London companies in the early 17th century. Thus, Derry, too, is a plantation town, which achieved the most celebrated moment in its history when it withstood a long siege in 1689 by the army of the Catholic James II, in his attempt to win back his lost throne. Today, Derry is the second most important city in Northern Ireland and it has been going through a process of rejuvenation in recent years.

NORTHERN IRELAND'S GLORIOUS COASTLINE

Derry, standing on the River Foyle which flows into Lough Foyle and onwards into the Atlantic Ocean, held a special place in the hearts of many of the people of Ulster in the 19th century, for

371

RIGHT: Hezlett House, located at Castlerock, near Coleraine, is a framed thatched cottage with an interesting cruck-truss roof construction dating from 1691.

OPPOSITE: Surfers at Castlerock on the north Derry coast.

PAGE 374 LEFT: The town hall in the market town of Coleraine, on the River Bann, County Derry, dates from 1743.

PAGE 374 RIGHT: Children at the Island Equestrian Centre near Coleraine.

PAGE 375 LEFT: Jeannie McCollum, co-founder with her husband, Lyle, of Island Irish Art in Coleraine, now one of Ireland's most prestigious galleries.

PAGE 375 RIGHT: The cannon known as Roaring Meg, that was used in the 1689 Siege of Derry, is located on the double bastion on Derry's 17th-century city walls – some of the best preserved in Europe.

OPPOSITE: Part of the now-ruined 18th-century Downhill Demesne is the circular Mussendon Temple, overlooking the Magilligan Strand at Benone, near Castlerock, Derry. It was the romantic vision of Frederick Hervey, Earl of Bristol and Bishop of Derry, who built the temple as his library, modelling it on the Temple of Vesta at Tivoli in Italy.

LEFT: The ruins of the Downhill Demesne, built by the Bishop of Derry.

PAGE 378: Magilligan Strand stretches for 8 miles (13km) to the Lough Foyle estuary. Inishowen, in Donegal, can be seen in the distance looking north-west from Bishop's Road.

PAGE 379: The sport of harness-racing is well-established in Ireland, with flat strands, like that of Magilligan, offering ideal conditions where trotting horses can be exercised.

RIGHT: Coastal drift and estuarine deposits from the River Foyle created the flat, fertile farmland of Magilligan, north of Limavady.

OPPOSITE: The Martello tower at Magilligan Point, at the narrow neck of the Foyle estuary, is a coastal defence left over from the Napoleonic Wars.

beautiful Mountains of Mourne, celebrated in poetry and song, reach down to the sea.

In between, there is something for everyone. Most spectacular on the northern coast is, of course, the Giant's Causeway, Northern Ireland's only World Heritage Site. The estimated 40,000 basalt columns (see page 352 et seq.), most of them hexagonal in shape, and of which it is composed, reach out from the cliffs of Antrim into the sea, pointing towards Scotland. It is so imposing that it is hardly surprising it should figure as greatly in the myths and legends of Ireland as it does in the textbooks of geologists.

ABOVE & OPPOSITE: The North West 200, Ireland's most famous international road race. The bikers are heading for Portstewart.

FAR RIGHT: Portrush's Victorian railway station, opened in 1855, was designed in a mock-Tudor style.

hundreds of families fleeing famine departed for North America from here. Their last sight of Ireland would have taken in the city, the lough and the coastline, indented and broken by rivers and sea loughs that gradually disappeared below the horizon.

Many of Northern Ireland's greatest scenic attractions are to be found along its coast, ranging from the golden sands of Benone Strand, Ireland's longest beach at the tip of Lough Foyle, right around to the Mourne coast, where County Down's

OPPOSITE: Sea angling at White Rocks, near Portrush on the North Antrim Coast.

LEFT & PAGES 386 & 387: The East Strand, great for walkers and surfers, runs along the edge of the Royal Portrush Golf Club, between White Rocks and Portrush.

PAGE 388: Looking west over White Park Bay – also popular with surfers – and the fishing village of Port Braddon to the Giant's Causeway headlands on the North Antrim Coast Road.

Further east are other points of interest, including the alarming Carrick-a-Rede rope bridge (page 328), slung 80ft (25m) above the sea near Ballintoy and much visited by tourists, and the market town of Ballycastle, whose famous Ould Lammas Fair still operates under a charter first granted in the 15th century. A 50-minute boat ride out to sea from Ballycastle and you arrive at Rathlin Island, called Raghery locally, where Bull Point at its

FAR LEFT: Looking east over White Park Bay, between Bushmills and Ballycastle, toward Rathlin Island.

BELOW: A Christmas part dance in the village pub, Rathlin Island.

OPPOSITE LEFT: The present Killyleagh Castle is an impressive private residence in the town of Killyleagh, rebuilt in 1850. The first Killyleagh Castle was built by John de Courcy, who arrived with the Normans in 1205, later marrying the daughter of the King of Man.

OPPOSITE RIGHT: Lough Cowey, at the southern end of the Ards Peninsula. The freshwater lake is a favourite place for boaters and fishermen.

LEFT: A plant shop in the town of Killyleagh, west of Strangford Lough.

PAGES 392–395: Mount Stewart, the 18th-century neo-Classical seat of the marquises of Londonderry on the shores of Strangford Lough. Besides the Temple of the Winds, its celebrated landscaped park has a Dodo Terrace and Shamrock Garden, with their statues of animals and topiaries.

OPPOSITE LEFT: Reconstruction of a Pennsylvania log cabin in the Ulster-American Folk Museum in County Tyrone, such as would have been used by 19th-century Ulster immigrants.

OPPOSITE RIGHT: The Celtic High Cross of Ardboe stands on a small hillock close to the western shore of Lough Neagh in County Tyrone.

LEFT: Cricket at Ballymagorry, Tyrone.

PAGE 398: Rain clouds crossing Lough Neagh, as seen from the Battery on the western shore near Coagh.

PAGE 399: The Beaghmore prehistoric stone circles in the Sperrin Mountains, County Tyrone, date from between 2000 and 1200 BC.

OPPOSITE: Harry Avery's Castle, overlooking the Strule valley south-west of Newtonstewart. Harry Avery was in fact Henry Aimbreidh O'Neill, who died in 1392. The castle is unusual in that it is of stone construction, located within what was pre-plantation Ulster at the time. Even more curious are the two towers that resemble a gate-house of an earlier century, similar to the one at Carrickfergus Castle, Co. Antrim.

FAR LEFT: The ancient earthwork ritual site of Tullaghhoge Fort, near Cookstown, Tyrone. It was later adopted as an inauguration site by the O'Neill chieftains.

LEFT: Cookstown, in County Tyrone. It was founded by planter Alan Cooke in 1609.

western tip is home to tens of thousands of seabirds, including puffins, kittiwakes and razorbills.

Northern Ireland's eastern coast, at its most magnificent in County Antrim, where the Glens of Antrim stretch towards the coast, three of them converging near Cushendall, also boasts some of the Province's most historic buildings. Two of the finest are the superbly preserved Carrickfergus Castle, whose massive

RIGHT: A mountain stream flowing through the lush valley of the River Roe near Dungiven below the Glenshane Pass, that bisects the Sperrin Mountains.

FAR RIGHT: The view south-west from Bishop's Road above Magilligan, north of Limavady.

OPPOSITE: Storm waves buffeting a horse and rider on Magilligan Strand at Benone, Derry.

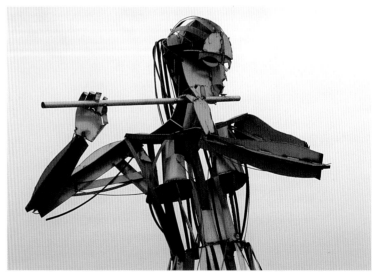

OPPOSITE LEFT: Coastal drift and estuarine deposits from the River Foyle built the long beach and flat farmland of Magilligan, north of Limavady.

OPPOSITE RIGHT & LEFT: Large semi-abstract metal figures of musicians illustrate the theme of Maurice Harron's, 'Let the Dance Begin', located on the Lifford Road between the border towns of Strabane and Lifford, County Tyrone.

PAGE 406: Looking east from Audley's Castle across the entrance of Strangford Lough to Portferry.

PAGE 407 LEFT: A dog rose (Rosa canis) blooming in the grounds of Audley's Castle, County Down.

PAGE 407 RIGHT: Audley's Castle, a tower house dating from around 1550.

keep dominates the harbour at Carrickfergus on the north shore of Belfast Lough and, further south on the Ards Peninsula overlooking Strangford Lough in County Down, Mount Stewart House.

The latter, dating mostly from the 19th century, has a wonderfully grand interior, but its great attraction is the superb

RIGHT: The southern shore of Strangford Lough, one of Europe's most important habitats for bird and marine species.

OPPOSITE: The late 18th-century Ballycopeland windmill, a local landmark near Millisle, has been restored to full working order, the miller's house and its associated buildings giving a unique insight into a lost industry..

PAGE 410: Low tide at Ballywalter, located on the Irish Sea coast of the Ards Peninsula between Donaghadee and Ballyhalbert.

PAGE 411: The yacht marina at Bangor, the largest in Ireland, at the north end of the Ards Peninsula.

OPPOSITE: Buildings from different centuries stand side by side in the resort of Bangor in County Down. The old tower was built as a Custom House in 1637.

LEFT: Castle Ward, a Georgian mansion built in two distinct architectural styles, Classical and Gothic. The 750-acre walled estate is located on the southern shore of Strangford Lough.

OPPOSITE: *The manor house of Springhill, a 17th-century plantation house in Ballydrum near Moneymore, County Londonderry. In addition to the house and its gardens, there is a costume collection and even a ghost! It has been the property of the National Trust since 1957.*

LEFT: *Giant gunnera (*Gunnera manicata*) in the ornamental gardens at Springhill. Commonly and erroneously called 'giant rhubarb', gunnera is one of the biggest and most spectacularly architectural of the herbaceous plants.*

PAGE 416: *Farmland in the rolling hills of County Down, west of the village of Clough.*

PAGE 417: *The Green Row cottages on the Castle Ward Estate.*

RIGHT & OPPOSITE: Exibits in the outdoor Ulster Folk and Transport Museum at Cultra, near Belfast, illustrating the traditions and way of life of the people of Northern Ireland in the early 20th century. It tells their story in 50 exhibits taken from all over Ulster, that have been carefully restored and authentically furnished.
Right: The Old Rectory.
Opposite above, left & right: The 19th-century Coshkib Farm, moved from Cushendall.
Opposite below left: Interior of the Old Rectory.
Opposite below right: The Corner Shop.

PAGE 420: The lighthouse on Donaghadee harbour on the Ards Peninsula, Down.

PAGE 421: The Castle Coole estate mansion near Enniskillen, Fermanagh, completed in 1798 for the Earl of Belmore.

Examples of antique lace and crochet work from the Sheelin Antique Irish Lace Museum at Bellanaleck, Fermanagh. The museum's curator is Rosemary Cathcart, pictured opposite right.

gardens in which the house is set. Created by Edith, Lady Londonderry in the 1920s, the gardens of Mount Stewart House (pages 393–395) are now rated among the finest in the United Kingdom. The house, once the home of the powerful Londonderry family, whose most famous scion was the British Foreign Secretary of the early 19th century, Lord Castlereagh, is now the jewel in the crown of the National Trust in Northern Ireland. Among its finest attractions are Stubbs's celebrated painting of the racehorse Hambletonian, which hangs in the house, and the lovely Temple of the Winds, built as a banqueting pavilion in 1785 in the grounds.

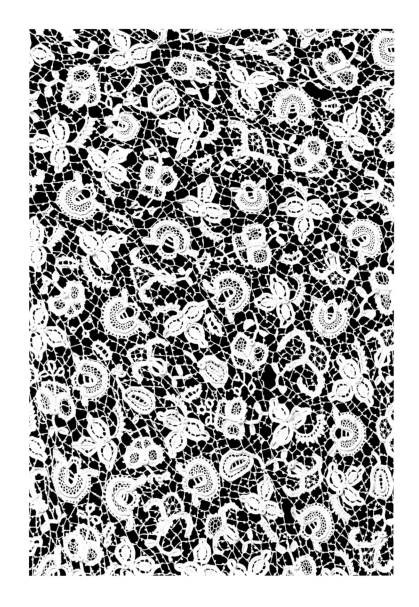

RIGHT: Cattle graze on limestone pasture below Cuilcagh Mountain, the summit of which spans south Fermanagh and Cavan.

OPPOSITE: Looking north-west over Lower Lough Erne from the Cliffs of Magho, Fermanagh, to Donegal.

Glenariff, one of the Nine Glens of Antrim and a perfect U-shaped valley, its rocky sides falling away to Waterfoot Beach.

Strangford Lough, largest of the sea loughs of Northern Ireland's eastern and southern coasts, is an area of considerable beauty with many places of interest. These include several castles clustered around its seaward end; the village of Saul, where St. Patrick is believed to have established his first church in Ireland; and, near its western shore, the fascinating pre-Norman monastic site of Nendrum on Mahee Island, one of nearly 120 islands in the lough.

FAR LEFT: Seaside villas in the resort town of Warrenpoint on the northern shore of Carlingford Lough in County Down.

LEFT: The Sperrin Mountains, County Tyrone, looking north over Gortin village in the valley of the Owenkillew river east of Newtownstewart.

PAGE 428: Looking north over Lower Lough Erne from the Cliffs of Magho towards the Blue Stack Mountains.

PAGE 429: A pleasure boat on Lower Lough Erne near Enniskillen, Fermanagh.

Strangford Lough comprises one of Europe's richest maritime habitats. Visit the lough in early summer and it is possible to see hundreds of common seals inhabiting the rocks and low reefs and, around the Narrows – the entrance to the lough – even a basking shark gliding through the water. There are also giant skate in the deep waters and great shoals of herring fry, too. The lough's prolific marine life naturally attracts great numbers and varieties of birds, with many kinds of migrating birds appearing on the lough in the early autumn.

RIGHT: Detail of a two-faced Janus figure standing in Caldragh churchyard on Boa Island, at the northern end of Lower Lough Erne. There is nothing quite like this 2,000-year-old figure anywhere else in Ireland.

OPPOSITE: The round tower and monastic buildings of Devenish Island, seen from the east shore of Lower Lough Erne near Enniskillen.

PAGE 432: The pretty fishing village of Strangford stretches along the southern shore of Strangford Lough where it narrows before meeting the sea. The Vikings, noting the strong tidal currents here, gave the place its name, meaning 'Strong Ford'.

PAGE 433: Only the ruins remain of Tully Castle, near Belleek in Co. Fermanagh, built by a planted family from Scotland in the early 17th century and destroyed and abandoned in 1641. Today it provides a fine backdrop for carefully tended gardens within the castle bawn.

THE PROVINCE'S INLAND GLORIES

Northern Ireland's coastline ends in the south on the shore of another great sea lough, Carlingford Lough. This, like others which indent the coast, leads naturally into the heart of the Province. Though primarily agricultural, with rolling green hills stretching as far as the eye can see, Northern Ireland is dominated, in fact, by some splendid stretches of water and, in its north-western corner, by a superb range of hills bisected by gloriously beautiful glens.

There are nine Glens of Antrim, carved by rivers cutting through the high plateaux of the Antrim Mountains. Left 'unplanted' by the English and Scots in the 17th century, the glens were for centuries wild and remote areas where the Gaelic language persisted for longer than anywhere else in Northern Ireland. Today, they are easily accessible from Antrim's fine coastal road, allowing thousands of visitors every year to enjoy the beauty of the scenery, much of the finest of which is enclosed within the Glenariff Forest Park. Glenariff, the best-known of the glens, was described by the novelist Thackeray as 'Switzerland in miniature', a description which still holds good. Glenariff village (also called Waterfoot) hosts a festival of Irish music each July.

The most prominent village in the glens is Cushendall, the 'Capital of the Glens', which sits below Glenballyemon, its streets creeping up the sides of the glen. Its most noticeable landmark is the Curfew Tower, built in 1809 as a prison for 'riotous persons'. For places of deeper historical significance, however, you should go

431

beyond Cushendall into Glenaan, where Ossian's Grave, a Neolithic court tomb named after Finn MacCool's son, lies beside a steep path up Tievebulliagh Mountain; or north a mile or so out of the village to Tiveragh, where an ancient mound, the Fairy Hill, is said to be a place frequented by the 'wee folk'; then on to Layde Old Church, founded by the Franciscans and an important burial place of the MacDonnell clan.

While nine rivers carved the Glens of Antrim, it took the waters of six rivers, including those of the Province's longest, the Bann, converging in the heart of Northern Ireland, to create Lough Neagh, the largest inland lake in the British Isles. At least, that's the geologists' story. Irish legend has it that the lake was created when Finn MacCool, picking up a piece of turf one day, hurled it into the Irish Sea, thereby leaving a large hole and creating the Isle of Man at the same time.

Since much of Lough Neagh is bordered by sedgy marshland, there are few roads along its banks and it has not become a great centre for watersports, though there is plenty of excellent fishing along the rivers which flow into it. The lough is most famous, in fact, for its eels, on which a thriving industry is based, with Toome, on the northern shore, having Europe's largest eel fishery.

Lough Neagh's most attractive recreational area is at its southern end. Oxford Island – really a peninsula – is home to an important nature reserve and bird-watching site. Further west, Peatlands Park is another excellent nature reserve with an

433

informative visitor centre, while Coney Island, near the mouth of the Blackwater and one of the few islands in Lough Neagh, belongs to the National Trust. Once a retreat for St. Patrick, the island is mainly visited today for its varied and abundant birdlife.

Travel further south and west through the Province and you come to a very different kind of lake scenery. Lower Lough Erne, a stretch of water covering much of the northern part of County Fermanagh and stretching, at its western edge, to within just a few miles of the Atlantic Ocean, has 97 islands scattered across it. One of the most important of these is Devenish Island, 3 miles (5km) from Enniskillen at the south-eastern end of the lough. St. Molaise founded a monastery on the island in the sixth century which remained an important religious centre for 100 years. Also well worth a visit are Boa Island, with its strange pre-Christian stone figures in Caldragh cemetery, and White Island, where extraordinary stone figures were set into the wall of an old monastery centuries ago.

Because this is an historically rich part of Ireland, a tour around Lower Lough Erne, taking in Enniskillen in the east and Belleek in the west, offers a splendid collection of historic and natural sites of interest. There are castles, such as the fortified plantation house, Tully Castle, on the southern shore of the lough; remote Monea Castle, a well-preserved plantation castle; and Enniskillen's famous castle, dating back to the 15th century and now a heritage centre and home to the Inniskillin Regimental Museum.

OPPOSITE: The corbelled turrets of Enniskillen Castle rise above the waterways which link Upper and Lower Lough Erne. Much of the small town of Enniskillen is built on an island in the waterway.

LEFT: A vintage sign advertising Guinness stout, in a street in Enniskillen.

PAGE 436: The fine Palladian-style Florence Court in Fermanagh is a beautifully maintained National Trust property, built in the 18th century by the Cole family, descendants of the planters of nearby Enniskillen.

PAGES 437 & 438: Florence Court's gardens are famous as the home of the Irish yew (Taxus baccata fastigiata), where the original tree, discovered in about 1760, can still be seen.

PAGE 439: Rose Cottage in the gardens of Florence Court.

435

There is a forest park, a country park, and the Lough Navar Scenic Route, a forest drive that leads to a superb viewpoint on the Cliffs of Magho on Lower Lough Erne's southern shore. From up here it is possible to see way over and beyond the waters of the lough to the Sperrin Mountains of Tyrone and the mountains of Sligo, Donegal and Leitrim.

Fermanagh's second largest lake is Upper Lough Erne, also dotted with islands and islets and surrounded by moorland country, broken into a patchwork of fields cut by rivers and smaller lakes, and marked by conifer plantations. The lovely River Erne, flowing north from Cavan and creating Upper Lough Erne in the process, is a link with the Irish Republic.

OPPOSITE: The lush farmland of the Roe Valley, County Derry.

LEFT: This rath in the Benedy Glen, Derry, dates back 1,500 years, being a fortified farmstead that was usually inhabited by one family. It protected farmstead, family and livestock from raiders.

INDEX